T0253184

Michel Ocelot

This unique book examines the career of Michel Ocelot, from his earliest works to his latest research and productions, including an interview regarding his latest film *Le Pharaon, le Sauvage et la Princesse* (2022). The book highlights the director's role in the panorama of contemporary animated cinema and his relationship with the tradition, both artistic and cinematographic.

The book carefully analyses the ethical and social nature of Ocelot's work to underscore the duality of the director's oeuvre, both artistic and social, using an interdisciplinary approach that blends film and aesthetic criticism with gender studies and decolonial thought. Particular attention will be given to the themes of multiculturalism, discrimination, and treatment of women, which are at the centre of many current cultural debates.

The book will be of interest to an audience of experts, animation enthusiasts, and film scholars, as well as to a wider readership interested in learning about the poetics of Kirikou's father.

Laura Buono holds a Master's degree in Visual Arts from Alma Mater Studiorum – Università di Bologna and completed a postgraduate course in Critical Theory of Society at the University of Milano-Bicocca, Italy. They are a minority rights activist and an independent researcher. They contributed to the drafting of *Animation: A World History* (2016) by Giannalberto Bendazzi. They participated in the production of national and international animation film festivals including Animadrid, Madrid International Animated Image Festival, Spain. They have been involved in the coordination and development of cultural outreach projects for several museums in Milan. They currently live and study in Rome, Italy.

The Focus Animation Series aims to provide unique, accessible content that may not otherwise be published. We allow researchers, academics, and professionals the ability to quickly publish high-impact, current literature in the field of animation for a global audience. This series is a fine complement to the existing, robust animation titles available through CRC Press/Focal Press.

Series Editor Chris Robinson is the Artistic Director of the Ottawa International Animation Festival (OIAF) and is a well-known figure in the animated film world. We welcome any submissions to help grow the wonderful content we are striving to provide to the animation community.

For more information about this series, please visit: https://www.routledge.com/Focus-Animation/book-series/CRCFOCUSANI

Michel Ocelot
A World of Animated Images

Laura Buono

CRC Press
Taylor & Francis Group
Boca Raton   London   New York

CRC Press is an imprint of the
Taylor & Francis Group, an **informa** business

First edition published 2024
by CRC Press
2385 NW Executive Center Drive, Suite 320, Boca Raton FL 33431

and by CRC Press
4 Park Square, Milton Park, Abingdon, Oxon, OX14 4RN

CRC Press is an imprint of Taylor & Francis Group, LLC

© 2024 Laura Buono

Reasonable efforts have been made to publish reliable data and information, but the author and publisher cannot assume responsibility for the validity of all materials or the consequences of their use. The authors and publishers have attempted to trace the copyright holders of all material reproduced in this publication and apologize to copyright holders if permission to publish in this form has not been obtained. If any copyright material has not been acknowledged please write and let us know so we may rectify it in any future reprint.

Except as permitted under U.S. Copyright Law, no part of this book may be reprinted, reproduced, transmitted, or utilized in any form by any electronic, mechanical, or other means, now known or hereafter invented, including photocopying, microfilming, and recording, or in any information storage or retrieval system, without written permission from the publishers.

For permission to photocopy or use material electronically from this work, access www.copyright.com or contact the Copyright Clearance Center, Inc. (CCC), 222 Rosewood Drive, Danvers, MA 01923, 978-750-8400. For works that are not available on CCC please contact mpkbookspermissions@tandf.co.uk

Trademark notice: Product or corporate names may be trademarks or registered trademarks and are used only for identification and explanation without intent to infringe.

Library of Congress Cataloging-in-Publication Data
Names: Buono, Laura, author.
Title: Michel Ocelot : a world of animated images / Laura Buono.
Description: First edition. | Boca Raton : CRC Press, 2024. | Series: Focus animation series | Includes bibliographical references.
Identifiers: LCCN 2023025184 (print) | LCCN 2023025185 (ebook) | ISBN 9781032272962 (hardback) | ISBN 9781032272993 (paperback) | ISBN 9781003292173 (ebook)
Subjects: LCSH: Ocelot, Michel--Criticism and interpretation. | Animated films--France--History and criticism. | Animators--France--Biography. | Motion picture producers and directors--France--Biography.
Classification: LCC NC1766.F82 O35 2024 (print) | LCC NC1766.F82 (ebook) | DDC 791.43/34094--dc23/eng/20230728
LC record available at https://lccn.loc.gov/2023025184
LC ebook record available at https://lccn.loc.gov/2023025185

ISBN: 978-1-032-27296-2 (hbk)
ISBN: 978-1-032-27299-3 (pbk)
ISBN: 978-1-003-29217-3 (ebk)

DOI: 10.1201/9781003292173

Typeset in Minion
by MPS Limited, Dehradun

Contents

Introduction

The idea for this book was born in Giannalberto Bendazzi's flat in Genoa, a few kilometres away from Michel Ocelot's birthplace. During one of our long chats, Giannalberto, with whom I had already collaborated over the years, asked me if I wanted to write a book for this series. We reasoned together about the potential themes to be explored and, after weighing up a few possibilities, he told me that a monograph on Ocelot's work had never been written before. Indeed, despite the prominent position occupied by the French filmmaker in the panorama of contemporary animated cinema, only short articles and reviews had been written up to that moment. A systematic survey of his work, considering the different aspects of his poetics, had not yet been carried out. Meanwhile, a significant exhibition has been dedicated to him, *Michel Ocelot: Artificier de l'imaginaire*, at the Musée-Château in Annecy, the catalogue of which is the most relevant contribution to the author's work (Figure I.1).

The reasons I chose to undertake this project are multiple. First, like many others of my generation, I had watched *Kirikou et la Sorciére* as a child and still have a very vivid memory of the impression it made on me at the time. Animated features and series have always been part of my everyday life; I knew Disney films by heart and watched a lot of anime, but the uniqueness of this film amazed me even back then. *Kirikou et la Sorciére*, was a groundbreaking movie; nevertheless, the widespread and well-deserved interest in this film often overshadowed the rest of his

DOI: 10.1201/9781003292173-1

FIGURE I.1   Michel Ocelot. © Ocelot-Studio O.

Without wishing to sound pretentious, I think I am like an apple tree bearing apples. The tree can't explain why it does so. Ever since childhood I have always been like that, wanting to amuse myself and others by creating things, making simple contraptions work and giving little gifts. [...]

I want to give pleasure by creating something beautiful and hopefully do some good at the same time, by sharing of thoughts and observations. [...] People have sometimes asked me what I would do if I were hugely rich: I would carry on doing exactly the same as I am doing today.

MICHEL OCELOT

filmography, which, given its complexity and innovative power, deserved a careful and extensive study. However, it is from *Kirikou et la Sorciére* that all my research started. Before embarking on this path, though, I carefully evaluated my enthusiasm for this project. More than twenty years after the release of the feature film, the debate on the issue of the representation of marginalised groups had developed enormously, and I wondered whether my enthusiasm for *Kirikou et la Sorciére* was also due to my position of privilege as a white person. Therefore, I questioned a number of racialised people on the subject, all of a similar age to me, who told me of their excitement at the time when seeing an animation so different from the norm for the first time in cinemas. One person, in particular, an Afrodescendant Italian, told me, "Kirikou changed my life!". It was then that I decided to start writing.

Second, I decided to devote attention to the filmmaker's work, as it would allow me to analyse his filmography from a visual and technical point of view while also applying a transdisciplinary approach, following in the footsteps of gender studies and decolonial thought. The reason for employing this perspective is determined by the strong social dimension of his work, an aspect that the author himself has often highlighted. In order for my perspective on Michel Ocelot's cinema to be fully understood, I began by positioning myself. I am a white, non-binary, and queer middle-class person who grew up in Italy in the 1990s. I am convinced that visual culture plays an active role in creating systems of power related to class, race, and gender. For this reason, too, I have tried to report as much as possible a plurality of viewpoints, keeping a decolonial and intersectional feminist perspective, which I consider the most suitable for the analysis of contemporary society and its cultural productions. In addition to the bibliographical documentation and interviews with the director, I conducted a thorough search of online sources, which enabled me to more easily reach the opinions of people from marginalised groups, those who have been discriminated against, or people from cultures that are the subject of representation in Ocelot's films. I have tried to report all the opinions, including the most critical views, which best shed light on the limitations of Ocelot's work as well. The result is an approach that I hope will be as open as possible to investigating the complexity of the issues involved.

The main aim of this volume is to take up the challenge of capturing Michel Ocelot in full and in all his complexity. The essay examines his entire career, from his earliest works to his latest research and productions, with particular attention to his poetics. I tried to delve into the director's working methods, while also exploring their layered aesthetic implications. The first chapter focuses on the biographical account of the director's early years and his first approaches to the world of animation. The central theme of this chapter is the analysis of *Les 3 Inventeurs*, his first independent production and a key work for understanding his entire filmography. It reveals his idea of art, cinema, and beauty, and it's a veritable declaration of his poetics. The second chapter focuses on the analysis of his silhouette films, a genre that was scarcely used in the past and that has stylistically oriented Ocelot's entire oeuvre. Indeed, the simplicity and clarity of silhouette films were guidelines for the director even when he chose to use other techniques. All his silhouette movies, whether made in *papier découpé* or created through computer graphics, are considered part of the same body of work. To assess their style and innovative features, these works are also compared with other silhouette films, particularly the work of the pioneer of this genre, Lotte Reiniger. The third chapter focuses on the production and making of *Kirikou et la Sorciére*. It deals with the many implications of the enormous success of the movie and its impact on French animation cinema. One section is dedicated to the reception of the movie by audiences and critics. It also analyses the modes of production and the narrative and visual characteristics of the two sequels, *Kirikou et les Bêtes Sauvages* and *Kirikou et les Hommes et les Femmes*. The fourth chapter is dedicated to *Azur et Asmar*. The chapter focuses mainly on analysing Ocelot's proposed version of the theme of otherness. These components of the author's poetics were examined from the concept of "Orientalism", a definition given by Edward Said in 1978 to the set of institutions created by Westerners to establish relations of force and control with the "Orient". The film it is also compared with Disney's renowned classic *Aladdin*, to show innovative traits and limitations of the director with respect to the vision of the so-called "Orient". The fifth and final chapter analyses *Dilili à Paris*. The film is examined both visually and in terms of narrative choices. The volume concludes with a short interview with the filmmaker regarding his latest work, *Le Pharaon, le Sauvage et la Princesse*. In this case, I preferred to refer directly to Ocelot's own words on a film that was released a few months ago and is still being distributed in various countries, convinced moreover that it is necessary to look at anything with a little distance and ponder it for some time to be able to analyse it at its fullest.

This book was born especially through the initiative of Giannalberto Bendazzi, his great enthusiasm and his enormous generosity. I met Giannalberto when I was at university, an encounter so dazzling that it partly changed the course of my studies and, consequently, the course of my life. CRC Press accepted my book proposal about a month before Giannalberto's unexpected passing in December 2021. For me, writing this book has thus taken on an additional meaning; since with his passing, I have not only lost an intellectual guide, but also a friend and a mentor. I have missed his guidance in these months. The writing of this volume was also possible thanks to the help and support of many people. First of all, a great deal of thanks goes to Michel Ocelot, for his enormous willingness to answer all my questions. I am also grateful to him for his patience, kindness, and accuracy. I thank Ocelot's assistant, Philippe Silvy, who helped me in obtaining the images. I thank Simran Kaur, who followed me as Editorial Assistant and Will Bateman, Commissioning Editor for Games and Animation at CRC Press, whose great enthusiasm and helpfulness I appreciated. I thank the production companies Les Armateurs and Nord-Ouest Films for their kindness in allowing me to reproduce images from the films they produced. My thanks also go to the Musées d'Annecy and the head of the animated film collections, Yaël Ben Nun, for the help and for granting the images. Thanks are also due to Denis Vidalie, who allowed me to use his photos. I thank Michel Ocelot's collaborators, Bénédicte Galup and Thierry Buron, who agreed to interviews, allowing me to enrich this volume.

I thank my large biological family, especially my mother, for the support and backing she has given me over the years. Special thanks go to my sister Eleonora, for constant intellectual discussion, advice, and careful revision of parts of the text. I thank Martina Bignamini, for the intense exchanges of ideas, which allowed me to deepen many reflections. I thank Pasquale Fameli, for valuable guidance and accurate advice; and Giacomo Tarascio, for the bibliographic suggestions. Thanks go to Ale/Sandra Cane and Noemino Novello, both of whom assisted me in the content and formal revision of some passages of the text. I thank my Milanese chosen family, without whom many of the reflections in the book would not have been possible, but especially for the mutual support, and for the time and experiences shared over the past years. For all the love, patience, joy, and much more, I thank Astro.

This book is dedicated to the memory of my father. Particularly because in my previous writing experiences his help and advice were invaluable, and I believe he could have made a difference in this case as well.

Rome, April 2023

CHAPTER 1

Ars Animativa

EARLY LIFE

Getting to know about Michel Ocelot's early life is not simple. He is a very private person and he prefers not to give a lot of information about himself, clarifying that he already expresses everything he has to say with his films. Maybe this is why he started to find amusing the mystery arising concerning his date of birth. Then, it became customary for the filmmaker not to reveal it. So, to respect his wishes, I have decided not to give a "when", but only a "where": Ocelot was born in Villefranche-sur-Mer, a small and pleasing town on a delightful bay near Nice, the region where he spent his infancy, in the 1940s.

In the 1950s the young Michel moved with his parents, his two brothers and his sister, to Conarky, in Guinea. Ocelot's parents were both primary school teachers, while his father was also a school inspector. As recalled by their son, they were truly devoted to their young students and were dedicated and passionate teachers with a progressive and inclusive concept of culture. Eager and enthusiastic travellers, they took their children from a young age on trips around the world. Although the French colonial experience in that African region was still in place, the parents of the future director made what was an unusual decision for those times, and they enrolled their children in a local country school – an experience that is very often

DOI: 10.1201/9781003292173-2

FIGURE 1.1 Childhood drawing by Michel Ocelot, 1950s. © Ocelot-Studio O.

remembered by Ocelot as an exceptional chance to get closer to the population and to the Guinean traditions. These five years spent in Guinea left an enduring mark on him, his childhood being "one of the most important parts of life"[1] in the process of forming his personal and artistic identity (Figure 1.1).

Moreover, the family returned every summer to the French Riviera to spend the holidays. Therefore, he had two completely different worlds at his disposal. He has described his childhood as happy and full of joy, the best a child could dream of, with loving parents, great siblings, and complete freedom, in addition to the exceptional environment in which he had the opportunity to grow up.

As the animator himself likes to recount, from an early age he was already training for what would be his future job: Since he was one and a half years old, he started to scribble, draw and play with pencils, paint, scissors, and paper. He amused himself by building imaginary worlds in which to make others play. He derived enormous pleasure from the delight of others. He applied his creativity to decorating the house and capturing with sketches the passers-by he saw while looking out of the window. It is also possible to trace his love for storytelling back to his childhood. Around the age of eight, he wrote illustrated stories to his grandmother, as proven by several letters full of intricate tales and drawings (Figure 1.2).

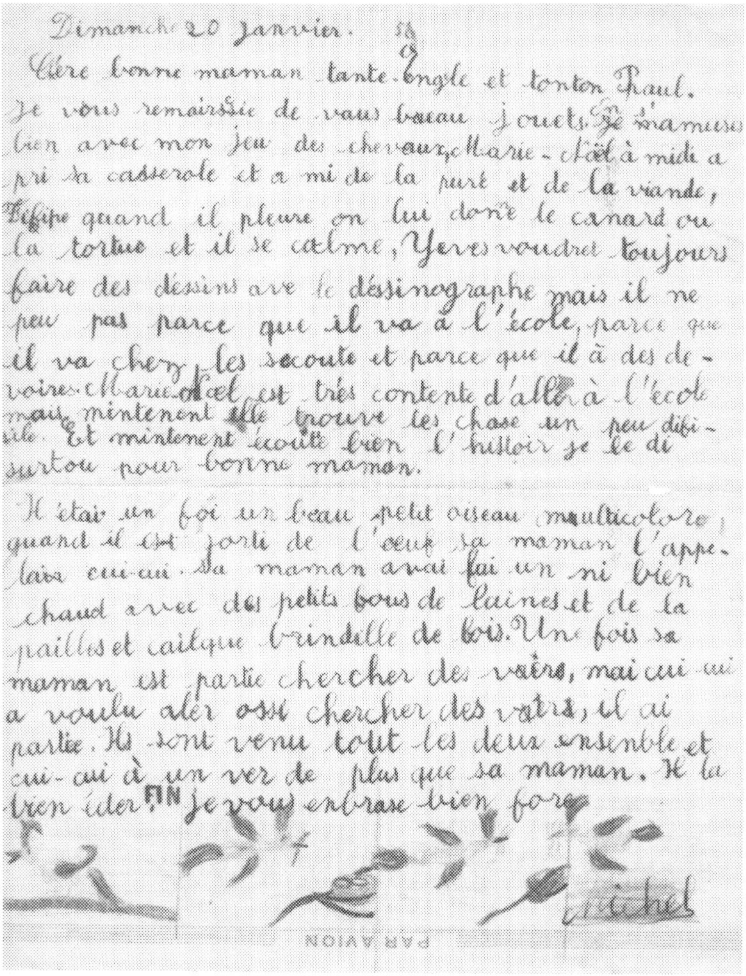
Dimanche 20 Janvier. 58

Chère bonne maman tante Angèle et tonton Paul.
Je vous remairsie de vaus beau jouets. Je m'amuse bien avec mon jeu des chevaux, Marie-Noël à midi a pri la casserole et a mi de la purée et de la viande, Pépipe quand il pleure on lui donne le canard ou la tortue et il se calme, Yves voudrai toujours faire des dessins ave le dessinographe mais il ne peu pas parce que il va à l'école, parce que il va chez les scouts et parce que il à des devoires. Marie-Noël est très contente d'aller à l'école mais mintenant elle trouve les chose un peu dificile. Et mintenant écoute bien l'histoir je le di surtou pour bonne maman.

Il était un foi un beau petit oiseau moulticolore, quand il est sorti de l'oeuf sa maman l'appelaiv cui-cui. Sa maman avai fai un ni bien chaud avec des petits bous de laines et de la pailles et quelque brindille de bois. Un fois sa maman est partie chercher des vers, mai cui cui a voulu aler ossi chercher des vers, il ai partie. Ils sont venu tout les deux ensemble et cui-cui à un ver de plus que sa maman. Il la bien ider. FIN je vous embrasse bien fort

michel

PAR AVION

FIGURE 1.2 Illustrated story by Michel Ocelot for his grandmother, 1950s. © Ocelot-Studio O.

Furthermore, it was probably in those days that he acquired a taste for paper theatre. His father liked to put on shows for the family in a cute toy theatre, with tiny characters and scenery in printed cardboard behind. The magic unleashed by these small theatre shows impressed Michel vividly, and, later, the same love of simple things permeated all his creations. He recalled:

> It was a little paper theatre: a castelet, and a curtain that rose, uprights, a set, and cut-out characters, sometimes coming from the vendors, sometimes made by my father. When, later, I started animation, I didn't think about the little paper theatre anymore. I only wanted drawn animation. The lack of money forced me to go back to this little paper world, but it also answered one of my wavelengths.[2]

It was also during his childhood, at the age of seven and just after a family and friends bash, that he had his first encounter with animation: Watching the 1946 Czech animated film *Vzpoura hraček* (*Revolt of the Toys*), by Hermína Týrlová. It thrilled him to such an extent that he grasped for the first time the great power of cinema and the animated image:

> Someone turned on a machine, a blinding light appeared, soon accompanied by a clicking sound. [...] There was a sheet stretched over the wall and on it, the image of a toy store. A real store, real toys like mine! And soon, those real toys started to move by themselves. Wooden soldiers start to parade, a fire engine comes out of its box, a small plane rolls on the ground and flies away! I am enchanted and there are two enchantments: A story that I understand well and on the other hand a certain intellectual excitement, real toys, which cannot move by themselves,

FIGURE 1.3   Michel Ocelot as a child. © Ocelot-Studio O.

start to live. I have been bitten for life by the innocent sorcery of animation, of the picture by picture work[3] (Figure 1.3).

After Ocelot's time in primary school in Guinea, his family returned permanently to France. At the age of twelve Michel found himself in Angers, a city in western France, which was, for him, a third unknown world, which he disliked because of the rain, the cold, and the big high school, a completely new experience after year-round sunshine and a small, quiet neighbourhood school. While still a teenager, he realised that animation could be his path, and he began making short films with his father's camera. Nevertheless, he soon had to deal with the absence of courses dedicated to animation. At the Ecole Régionale des Beaux-Arts in Angers, he had the chance to experiment with many mediums and learn different techniques. Hence, he started to think that animated films would allow him the scope to draw, to cut, to paste, to tell stories and to engage with anything that teased his imagination. Animation became an answer to all those who told him that dividing his time into so many activities wouldn't get him anywhere. At the time, Michel was experimenting with every expressive means available. He wrote a lot, drew, painted, and sculpted; he did embroidery, theatre, mime, and dance. He liked reading and going to theatre shows and to the cinema. Animation, with its multidisciplinary nature, seemed an ideal occupation for someone who mastered so many skills and cultivated all these passions.

Thereafter, Michel moved to Paris to attend the Ecole Nationale Supérieure des Arts Décoratifs and, with disappointment, found out that the courses were largely concentrated on interior design. There was very little graphic art and no trace of animation. In both academies, he asked for a Department of Animation and each of them opened one – only after he left. In this period, he spent a good part of his time devoting himself to drawing. His works of those years already show a great attraction to clean, sinuous lines. His interest in illustration and graphics led him to intricate decorative motifs and strong contrasts that would later become a distinctive feature of his films. He likewise discovered the power of the great clarity and incisiveness of profile representation, an element that would become recurring and pervasive in his cut-out animations.

Michel's various attempts to find his way in the world of animation through artistic training courses carried out in Europe were not successful. At the end of the 1960s, it was necessary to go overseas to really grasp the secrets of animation. On one hand, Ocelot didn't dream of being like Walt Disney or working for Disney's studios, and he tended to despise Mickey Mouse. However, he wanted to learn as much as he could, and he wanted to reach the homeland of animation, the United States. Thanks to a scholarship he won, he was able to apply to a Los Angeles academy, The Art Center College of Design, in 1968, and thereafter to The California Institute of the Arts, the school that had trained some of Disney's most talented animators. He enjoyed his time in these schools, but, despite his young age, he already had very clear ideas about his future. He wasn't interested in classic animation at all and the commercial blockbuster film industry wasn't for him. He knew his path was oriented towards independent, authorial, high-quality animation. Ocelot brought with him a highly elaborate and audacious portfolio of creations, which left everyone amazed by its complexity, sophistication, and quality.[4] Clearly, commercial animators were capable of dealing with the production of extremely complex projects, unimaginable for Ocelot, but his style was already recognisable and ready to blossom into something great. After one year in Los Angeles, Ocelot came back to do his military service at the Établissement cinématographique des armées (Armed Forces Film Establishment) where he made animated movies that, due to military secrecy, could not be shown elsewhere. Afterwards, he was hired by a small company to make animated movies, but orders for these movies never arrived. Eventually, he had to quit the job. During that time, he carried out his first experiments with a 16 mm camera:

> they were really amateur films, without sound, without having any expertise and without knowing how it was done. [...] I had a projector that never worked at a regular speed. So I never knew the result of my animations! As the projector heated up, it would speed up.[5]

Ocelot shot some short films on his own, but with long intervals between them, and this was the beginning of a long period of inactivity. He worked for two years in the field of graphics, but no animation studio would take him on.

FIRST TELEVISION PRODUCTIONS: *GÉDÉON*

In 1975 Ocelot had his first fruitful encounter with a film producer, Yves Rousset-Rouard, who at that time intended to invest the money earned from the success of his first live-action movies in setting up an animation studio. Rousset-Rouard was already fairly established economically, so he organised a contest to look for new scriptwriters – the making of a short film to warn of the dangers of cardiovascular diseases – and noticed Ocelot's work. Even though Ocelot was still an amateur, Rousset-Rouard decided to ask the young artist to take care of his first animation production, *Gédéon*, with which he would have a central role and great responsibility, being at once author, scriptwriter, storyboarder, model maker and director (Figure 1.4).

Gédéon (*Gédéon*) was an animated television series, with sixty episodes of five minutes each, broadcast from 9 February 1976 on TF1. It was an adaptation for television of the comic strip *Gédéon* by the illustrator and comic book artist Benjamin Rabier,

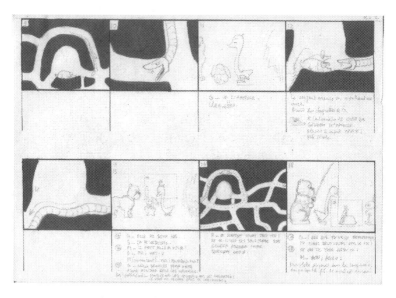

FIGURE 1.4   Gédéon storyboard, 1976. © Ocelot-Studio O.

created in 1923 and published between the two World Wars by Editions Garnier Frères. Gédéon is a yellow duck who is rejected by everyone on the farm where he was born because of his unusually long neck. He decides to run away to the countryside. There, he starts to make many friends among the small countryside animals, whom he helps to overcome some difficulties, thanks to his cleverness.

Ocelot had little knowledge of animation at the time and therefore chose a method that would be both the simplest and the most entertaining. The appealing character's design is very simple and the animation was realised with a combination of traditional cel technique and paper cut-out.

> I decided to make Gédéon in mixed media, essentially paper cut-outs animated under camera, accompanied by phases where one position of a cut-out character is replaced by another, so that he moves endlessly. I was aware of the enormity of traditional animation [...] you need a lot of people. You also need a lot of space. and I said to myself, we can't afford so many people, it's dangerous and moreover it's boring. It's nobody's baby, it's a bit dehumanised and I thought I'd rather do some handicraft work to make it more interesting[6] (Figure 1.5).

This first commission was an opportunity for an initial approach to animation and to establish a working method. First, the drawn characters were created. Once completed, the articulated paper figures, obtained by overlapping elements that were cut out and then reassembled, were placed on the backgrounds. In subsequent films, the production process would always be the same, readjusting and developing it according to need. The use of *papier découpé* allowed the director and his collaborators to animate the characters in far fewer steps, using limbs, beaks, ears, and wings that could be easily articulated. Some of these devices anticipated the techniques that would be largely employed for

FIGURE 1.5 Gédéon animation phase on set. Paper cut-out, ink and watercolour on paper, 1976. © Ocelot-Studio O / Photo Credit: Denis Vidalie.

movies that would follow. Gédéon and another main character, Sosthène, the rabbit, could radically change expression thanks to simple paper cut-out eyes, that could be placed in different positions according to necessity, a cunning device that easily solved the problem of possible deformation in the drawing once animated, in addition to giving elegance and essentiality to the figures, all strictly bi-dimensional. The figurines of the characters and the decorations composing the backgrounds were covered on the back side with black cardboard so that they could be lighted from behind or turned the other way around to film the night scenes. In this way, the figures and the scenery would appear as dark silhouettes on a coloured light background, with the same fascinating simplicity of some future Ocelot's creations. The backgrounds are a remarkable component, impressive in refinement and sophistication. The plants and the flowers, especially, served as an elegant and captivating setting. Their design is a clear reference to nineteenth-century graphics. The influence of late nineteenth-century visual imagery of French and English provenance decorations, inspired by nature, is distinctly noticeable and would continue to fascinate the artist in later years. He would return to these frequently.

Gédéon was Ocelot's first official work as a professional director. Rousset-Rouard, who had a sincere interest in animated films, decided to set up an animation studio from scratch in Neuilly-sur-Seine, but everything came to an end shortly after: An altercation over the working conditions of the studio subordinates ended the experience. The studio closed and the producer continued to work successfully in live-action filmmaking, never again employing animators. Ocelot lost an opportunity, but from this loss, he drew the motivation to finally find his way into independent animated filmmaking.

LES 3 INVENTEURS: A DECLARATION OF POETICS

Once this first brief adventure was over, the filmmaker decided it was time to show the world that he existed and that he could craft beautiful things. In a recent interview, Ocelot recounted his first time at the Annecy Festival, stating, "*I didn't talk to anyone and no one talked to me. I was all alone, unknown, I hadn't made any films*".[7] He was at the beginning of his career and he wanted to prove his talent. He decided to stop accepting small commissions and, with the money earned from *Gédéon*, he started a new project, his first independent and completely original film: *Les 3 Inventeurs* (*The 3 Inventors*), a thirteen-minute-long film about a family of three inventors: Mother, father, and daughter. The three are capable of building incredible machines, but the neighbours reject their inventions and their extravagant way of life to the point of persecuting them and burning all their possessions – until a reassuring voice reminds us that everything is happening only in cinematic fiction (Figure 1.6).

FIGURE 1.6 "La grande inventrice" from *Les 3 Inventeurs*. Bas-reliefs on scenery. Paper and paper cake doily, 1979. Musée-Château d'Annecy collection. Photo Credit: Denis Vidalie.

This movie, released in 1979, is a key work to understand the entire Ocelot's oeuvre, as it reveals his idea of art, cinema, and beauty. It is a veritable declaration of his poetics. First and foremost, it is certainly possible to identify the intentions of the director – a desire to be part of an artistic tradition that made craftsmanship one of its main traits. These objectives are made explicit by his statements regarding the film:

> I started *Les 3 Inventeurs* with the idea it will be my masterpiece and this mainly with a special meaning. I made it in the spirit of the Compagnons Ouvriers who at the end of their apprenticeship made a masterpiece, an extremely well-made object, rather complicated, something that you do once in a lifetime and then put it under a glass case to be admired.[8]

The animator makes use of the term "masterpiece" in a sense derived from the original meaning in French, the locution *chef-d'oeuvre*, adopted in the Middle Ages in the context of regulations concerning professional guilds of artisans. It was customary for an apprentice, once having completed his training in a master's workshop, to make a so-called masterpiece to prove his competence, thereby becoming an actual member of the guild. The successful completion of the task qualified him to practice as a full master.

Ocelot's description of his first independent film as a *chef-d'oeuvre* clearly brings out the extent to which the recovery of the craft dimension was a fundamental prerequisite for affirming his artistic and cinematic conception, thus finding his position within the coeval animation cinema through this vision. The production of *Gédéon* was harshly criticised for its lack of typical studio organisation, which would have a well-defined structure and a sort of assembly line, with an ordered set of tasks undertaken by designers, animators, painters, and other professionals. Ocelot refused that procedure and preferred an artistic approach; the storyline and the highly crafted quality of the new film stood adamantly at odds with the dominant film industry. He decided to stay alone and silent for one year, working exactly as he had always dreamt – independently, slowly and painstakingly.

Resuming a traditional artistic praxis also meant setting his work in opposition to a hegemonic way of producing in the panorama of world animation by reconnecting the threads with early cinema. The director's own words confirm his attachment to the original cinema, and his intentions to recreate the same genuine astonishment generated through the handcrafted construction of fantastic sets and phantasmagorical sceneries, realised despite skimpy budgets and very little equipment:

> It is Georges Méliès who made me want to become an animation filmmaker. But if I had started at the same time as the computer era I most probably would have

not made any movies, because there is not enough craftsmanship. And this is how I came to it by playing as a child with pencils, paint, paper, scissors. [...] He made cheerful movies, movies that make you want to do films yourself, with all that craftsmanship that I love.[9]

In fact, as pointed out by Michael Chanan, the aesthetic qualities of the early films were conditioned by the peculiarity of cinema as a new medium, which, unlike other new technologies, had inserted itself at the bottom of the market instead of at the top. The aesthetic conditions of early cinema were influenced by the scarcity of means available to directors and crews before cinema was absorbed and capitalised upon by a system that established more efficient production relations apt to intensify the economic exploitation of the new industry.[10] In this regard, Chanan cites Claude Levi Strauss's definition of *bricoleur* in his book, *The Savage Mind*, as a person who uses his hands but has inadequate means at his disposal compared with those of a craftsman. The description fits rather closely with the operation carried out by Ocelot for his little debut masterpiece. Sébastien Denis likewise emphasises the extent to which this artisanal and authorial dimension would become a trademark of French animation, the so-called "French Touch", namely an intellectual cartoon with "simple imagery, with refined graphics where the author's logic takes precedence",[11] characterised by a slow pace as opposed to cartoon-esque effectiveness.

The craft dimension of the director's early works is further enhanced by the utilisation of *papier découpé*, a technique "that favours direct animation,"[12] since the animator himself manipulates the various elements during the shooting. Cutout silhouette animation was a relatively infrequently employed technique in animated films. The young filmmaker chose this technique for its low production cost and ease of manipulation, after seeing the outstanding results while experimenting with it during animation workshops with children. The whole film was made entirely with paper cutouts and with dozens and dozens of white clippings of paper from start to finish. To achieve an effect recalling the refinement of the decorative arts of eighteenth-century France, Ocelot made use of pastel colours for the backgrounds, which were made from simple coloured cardboard, without any colour gradients or patterns. Over these, he placed cut-out and folded paper figurines, animated in two different modes: In some cases, the filmmaker preferred to cut out different versions of the same silhouette, changing some of its details to show the progression of action. Each figurine was then placed in an advanced position with respect to the previous one, in order to create the illusion of movement (Figure 1.7).

In most cases, animation is obtained via the traditional method already used by Lotte Reiniger, the pioneer artist who inspired Ocelot with her early silhouette films. In Reiniger's films, the small figures were similar to tiny puppets, made of cardboard or thin lead sheets, with articulated joints to connect the movable parts, which could be easily animated for filming by camera shots, as is the case in stop-motion animation. Ocelot improved on the original technique, adding tiny hinges, magnets, and springs to the paper cutouts, which avoided taping the figures for each shot and sped up the animation process. The figures in *Les 3 Inventeurs* had a microscopic structure of wires and bits of metal hidden in the back, a small trick that permitted them to be firmly held to the cardboard used as a stand, which was placed on top of a magnetic paper, instrumental for making resistance and not losing the preset positions. Such a system also detached the figurines slightly from the background, making them cast their own shadows and giving them depth and thickness, achieving the bas-relief effect that the author sought.

Using paper meant not only cutting and shaping, but playing with the material by engaging in a series of amusing operations such as folding and actually sculpting, achieving delicate chiaroscuro effects with different textures, and taking full advantage of the quality of the material. Working with paper was also a way

FIGURE 1.7 *Les 3 Inventeurs* animation phases, 1979. © Ocelot-Studio O / Photo Credit: Denis Vidalie.

for the animator to refer back to his own childhood, when he loved to decorate the house with patterned paper cutouts and tailor small gifts, created with white sheets of paper, for his mother. The *Les 3 Inventeurs* figures and objects were created by combining simple white paper and cake doilies, masterfully composed in order to achieve the typical embroidery-like effects of Rococo stucco decorations, a composition of various shades of whites on pastel blue or pink background. The ultimate outcome achieved a precise but richly nuanced aesthetic. The director wanted to create something exquisite, and in the art of the 1700s, he found characters with the harmony and vivid decorativism that he was looking for. Formal consistency is further reinforced by the use of silhouettes, which appeared as an art form in eighteenth-century France, a period that Ocelot chose precisely for its evocative power and refined taste, but also because it is considered a particularly favourable age in French history, as well as "a time when many new discoveries and inventions were made".[13]

For the creation of all the paper cuttings, which took him five months to complete, Ocelot didn't avail himself of any collaborator, and neither did he do so for the filming and the animation, which was realised in another three months. This slow and meditative work, carried out in absolute silence and complete solitude, was for the author a source of profound joy and great satisfaction. His desire and need for isolation were further aided by the production company's choice of location for the film shooting. The short development took place in a house lost in the mountains where Jean-François Laguionie, a prominent figure in independent animation in Europe and greatly admired by the novice animator, set his studio La Fabrique. The film was produced by a very small company, aaa production (Animation Art graphique Audiovisuel), created in 1973 by the producer Marcelle Ponti-Rouxel, the author-director Jacques Rouxel, and the director Jean-Paul Couturier. The company chose right from the start to favour culturally and artistically relevant cinematographic products and decided to support many fledgling artists. It is still active today. Nonetheless, the generosity and interest of the producers did not ease the difficulties that arose due to the very sparse equipment they were able to provide: An old camera without a viewfinder and with no automatic focus, viewer, or pegs, and very hard to move. Instead of a viewfinder, in order to define the field according to the camera's height, a big celluloid sheet was positioned on the table. Ocelot recalled, "Keeping the rig in place involved a pile of books, a broomstick suspended from the ceiling, attached with strings to lights [...], a weighted plank and an ancient iron".[14]

Since there was no automatic focus, every time Ocelot changed the position of the camera up or down, he had to adjust the focus for the new shot. One of the many times he forgot to do it, he continued to shoot in the same conditions until the entire work on the first film reel was finished. As the shooting location had no equipment to screen the movie, it was not possible to view and correct potential errors:

> I only discovered the problem after the job was done and the film spool had been transmitted to the lab [...] I had to go to a nearby city, in the cinema, where the projectionist screened my film with old noisy equipment. I had to identify and record all the problems in only two viewings.[15]

Moreover, the absence of a focus viewer made it much more difficult to shoot some sequences involving multiple superimpositions, such as the scene of the hot air balloon surrounded by the flock of birds, which required a high number of takes. This was an additional obstacle for a beginner who still had very little knowledge of the techniques.

Punctuated by these many difficulties, the undertaking was finally completed and the work had been made entirely of paper. The decision to employ *papier découpé* seemed almost a duty to the young film director, allowing him on the one hand to conduct technical experimentations and play with the material, and on the other to make a statement against those who had harshly criticised him while he was working on *Gédéon*, and who had said that cut-out animation was for amateurs. Thus Ocelot decided to show paper in all its materiality. Paper is by no means masked by the use of colour or drawing. On the contrary, it is shown in its crisp whiteness and artificiality. The paper was cut, folded, modelled and, on the screen, even destroyed. Moreover, the evidence of the material allowed the animator to enact the unravelling of the fictional device of filmmaking. At the end of the film, the metacinematic scene further confirms this willingness to reason on the nature of the filmic product. As would be the case with later films, the artifice is clearly visible and deliberately displayed to the viewer. As noted by Robert Stam,[16] self-reflexive strategies can make use of different resources, depending on the medium. While in literature we have purely verbal tools, in cinema the strategies can be multiple, going along with the nature of its multitrack sensorial construct. In the case of this animated film, the role of the self-reflexive device is entrusted to the material.

The direct interventions on paper play the role of unveiling the dual nature of the material. By showing the materiality of the medium through the exploration of the double function of the material as a fictional and disclosive tool of physical reality, an overturning from fiction to physicalness takes place: The universe created by Ocelot is not relegated to pure fiction, but it ennobles the screen as another reality. In *Les 3 Inventeurs,* the mimetic relationship with reality is completely negated by the choice and the display of an anti-naturalistic and explicitly artificial material, obtaining a deliberately exaggerated contrived appearance. Nonetheless, the linearity of the script, the sound effects, and the editing, together with the physicality and three-dimensionality of the paper figurines create a bond, an emotional one, with the spectator. When, at the end of the short, the house of the three protagonists begins to burn, the viewer's interpenetration is complete and it is there that the director intervenes with a metacinematographic scene: "Watch well. It's cinema!" The narrator reveals to us the filmic fiction precisely when the fire reveals the materiality of the paper. The ending emphasises a process that had already begun with the fire, which, by bringing the paper back to its most opaque materiality through destruction, discloses to us the fictional device. In this way the material performs a double function: Fictional throughout the unfolding of the story, and revelatory in the reversal from fiction to physicality, exposing its artifice in the final sequences. In the slow burning of the paper, the last scenes of the short film remain suspended between narrative and material dimensions. As the paper burns there is a gradual opening towards the physical reality of things, completed by the metalinguistic conclusion, which interrupts the narrative flow in order to foreground the specific means of filmic production. By creating a playful relationship with the norms and conventions of cinematic narrative, it succeeds in demystifying our unshakeable faith in fiction.

The film applies a self-reflexive strategy of folding in on itself, creating a veritable narrative origami. This emphasis on the metanarrative dimension has been read by Yaël Ben Nun as a willingness to question the mechanisms and structure of the traditional tales, thereby questioning the very society from which they originated.[17] The employment of a narrative structure derived from the fairy tale and the insistence on the figure of the narrator are in fact some of the expedients the filmmaker would also resort to in later works.

Ocelot is the author of the screenplay, a philosophical fable about creation and the genius's difficulties in integrating with a violent society. The protagonists are inspired by the life of chemist and scientist Antoine de Lavoiser and Marie-Anne Pierrette Paulze, his collaborator and wife. The director decided to take inspiration from them because this allowed him to stage a pair of scientists in which male and female figures played an equally important role in the development of their scientific research. The choice had also fallen on Lavoiser because he was condemned to death in the period of executions following the French Revolution. Although the chemist had been convicted for his role as a tax collector and not for his scientific activity, Ocelot chose him as a symbol of a knowledgeable figure whose intellectual value was scarcely recognised and who fell victim to the blindness of political extremism. The entire narrative architecture is influenced by the nineteenth-century romantic concept of a genius as a personality capable of transferring their own disruptive subjectivity into the work, which becomes a material extension of their interiority and, therefore, the result of a highly individual action. Such a creative act, generated in complete solitude and sheltered from the outside world, but directed towards its improvement, struggles to be accepted by the prejudiced and suspicious community. The story, therefore, becomes a self-narrative of Ocelot's own work. The atmosphere of wonder in the first part takes on extremely sombre tones towards the end of the short, only to be lightened in the finale, by the metacinematic insert, which plays down the seriousness of the entire story. Ocelot also plays on the contrast between form and content: Formal refinement, visual elegance and sophisticated taste imprinted on the entire work intervene to effectively enhance the harshness of the storyline. The beauty and delicacy of the scenery, the sense of wonder, and the aesthetic satisfaction experienced up to the moment of the aggression intensify the disquiet due to the plot, leaving a sense of subtle bewilderment after it is viewed.

The whole film is permeated with extreme delicacy and lightness. It is conceived as a small object of craftsmanship with a strong aestheticising purpose, making it a true statement of intent, where the search for and worship of beauty is not only a pivotal element in the conception and development of the short film, but it is part of a broader aspiration that runs through his complete body of works. Théophile Gautier, known to be the founder of the "art for art's sake" literary theory, wrote, "What is it for? – It serves to be beautiful, is that not enough? – Like flowers, like perfumes, like birds, like everything that man has not been able to divert and deprave to his own use".[18] Ocelot follows this principle throughout his entire oeuvre, making refinement and magnificence one of his distinctive features.

At first glance, some stylistic choices could appear artifactual and affected, due to the extreme insistence on the more purely ornamental aspects of an architectural and decorative style – eighteenth-century French Rococo – which is, in turn, contrived and redundant. The risk of slipping dangerously into kitsch is prevented by careful calibration of several high- and low-aesthetic touchstones, in addition to the compelling storyline, enriched with humanitarian and philosophical messages. As pointed out by Giannalberto Bendazzi, the short film walked the razor's edge between the ridiculous and the marvelous.[19]

The short movie is the manifestation of a refined preciosity with highly cultured references, from Luca Della Robbia's glazed terracottas to Donatello's sculptures, considered above all for their formal values and stylistic suggestion. The works of Luca Della Robbia, inventor and undisputed master of Renaissance glazed terracotta, are chosen for their visual qualities. Ocelot's interest in these artworks is due to their formal features. The director exploited the delicate contrast between the blue of the background, the whiteness of the figure, and the pictorial and luministic nature of this sculptural genre, which approximates the two-dimensionality and chiaroscuro effects of painting and drawing. This predilection accords with the choice of the cut-out technique, eminently oriented towards two-dimensionality and particularly suited to the author's synthetic style. The same may be said for Ocelot's preference for Donatello's stiacciato[20] over his other sculptures. The stiacciato is a very low relief intended to give a reduction in perspective of the real volume of bodies, therefore achieving pictorial value and low three-dimensionality. Moreover, the framing that characterises Renaissance figurative arts, especially Donatellesque stiacciato, is particularly well-suited to the employment of silhouettes.

In the movie, many scenes are enclosed in an elaborate paper frame. Camera movements are reduced due to the spatial limitations from the two-dimensionality of the technique and motions play out almost exclusively in the fixity of a frame or in the movement from one side of the screen to the other. Outstanding results were obtained by merging these visual sources with an accurate study of French Rococo art. Renaissance sculpture was chosen for its composure and sobriety to clear the Rococo of its utmost complexity, obtaining an effect of clearness and simplicity, despite its great sophistication.

Paper was also employed to obtain the sound effects. Robert Cohen-Solal, the musician in charge of sound effects, employed only paper for the entire film, with the exception of the sound of the bell. Christian Maire, the music composer, who had already worked with the director and whose contribution would become one of the most relevant and powerful of his first films, also played with simple mechanics. He employed instruments such as the harpsichord, widely played in the 1700s, and the celesta, a nineteenth-century musical instrument that allowed him to add a romantic and dreamy flavour to the soundtrack. There was the ingenious idea to place a microphone inside the wooden instruments, that, instead of hiding all the mechanical noises, would amplify these unusual sounds. For the dubbing of the voices, the filmmaker asked actor Michel Elias to participate, while Ocelot himself lent his velvety, calm voice to the narrator.

The remarkable result attracted notice from critics, who awarded it numerous prizes including a BAFTA for Best Animated Film at the British Academy of Film and Television Awards held in London in 1981 – a prize very rarely awarded to a French author – and the Golden Trophy at the International Film Festival of Odense in Denmark in 1980. Moreover, *Les 3 Inventeurs* won the First Prize at Animafest in Zagreb in 1980. Ocelot described this award as "a delicious memory, the first of my trophies and the happiest, unforgettable one".[21] That same year, Yuri Norstein's *Skazka Skazok* (*Tale of Tales* – 1979), which was chosen many times by critics over the years as the best-animated film of all time, won the Grand Prix at the Croatian festival. Ocelot recounted:

> The process was repeated in several festivals, both films in the same events with the same distinctions: Tale of Tales getting the Grand Prix and Les 3 Inventeurs the next prize. But I was happy, because I was in love with Tale of Tales and I needed, needed to see it again. The chance of festivals was the only possibility at that time to find it again.[22]

From the 1970s, one of the main goals for Western Europe animators was to distinguish their work from Disney's modus operandi. A viable alternative could be found on the other side of the Iron Curtain, but Ocelot considered many of these films too harsh and too bare. On the other hand, Norstein's delicacy and thoughtfulness had left him stunned.

Ocelot's first film had achieved its purpose. The director had entered the world of independent animation with his little masterpiece. Awards flattered him and pushed him to continue with even more determination, but his main aim at the time was to hire a studio. This achievement would be long in coming, although, thanks to his new connections and the support gained from this first independent work, he was slowly finding his way in the world of animated films.

LA LÉGENDE DU PAUVRE BOSSU

Completing Les 3 Inventeurs had been a complex and challenging undertaking. It required intense work, dainty to the extreme, but for Ocelot it also meant establishing a lasting collaboration with the aaa Production company, which commissioned him to make two films: Les Filles de l'Egalité (The Daughters of Equality), a dry-humoured one-minute movie, and the corporate short film *Beyond Oil*, both produced in 1981. In the same period, the company also produced the new short that Ocelot was working on, *La Légende du Pauvre Bossu* (*The Legend of The Poor Hunchback*), which was released in 1982. It won a César Award for Best Animated Short Film in 1983 and gained more attention from critics.

La Légende du Pauvre Bossu was conceived to have a diametrically opposite aesthetics to *Les 3 Inventeurs*, where Ocelot had focused on the refinement and complexity of the details, taking great care of every aspect personally and dedicating months of intense work. On the contrary, the new project was born with the intention of making it deliberately bare. The entire short was created with the use of simple felt-tip pen on white paper. Then the drawing was greyed with charcoal and pastel, and the light effects were attained by wiping it with a chammy cloth or an eraser. Besides these differences from *Les 3 Inventeurs*, *La Légende du Pauvre Bossu* can't be considered to be a typical traditional animation either, as for almost its entire duration there are only a few colours, very little animation, and no camera movement. The characters are just laid onto the backgrounds and the entire film maintains the straightforward and intuitive structure of an animatic. The figures and the few movements were obtained, once again, with a cut-out technique, but it would be impossible to tell this just by looking at it. Despite the lack of technical sophistication and rudimentary animation, the final result showed once more that even with simple means it was possible to achieve excellent results. Ocelot has often expressed his preference for a well-conceived narrative rather than for the smoothness of animation. Here it is particularly visible, as the rudimentary animation is supported by a solid storyline and thorough aesthetic research, which will become a hallmark of the artist in feature films. Moreover, with this short film the animator affirmed once more what he had already put into practice before, and would continue to uphold even when he switched to 3D animation: His total disregard for realism, a point that placed him in antithesis to Walt Disney's poetics. In this context, the choice to give limited movements to the figures can in fact achieve a greater aspect of veracity than the spasmodic search for hyperrealism typical of classic animated cinema. As Dick Tomasovic pointed out, "On closer observation, what animation gives the figure's body in movement, dynamics, energy, naturalism, and vitality, it loses in authenticity, naturalness, and original identity. The more it seems alive, the more it reminds us that it is an illusion".[23] This crucial aspect is particularly evident in this work and can be seen in all of his early productions. All of them are marked by the limited use of camera movements and animation restricted by the absence of economic resources but are not incapable of creating a coherent narrative universe and a credible filmic space. In addition, as was the case with his previous film, these features are combined with well-considered aesthetic choices aimed at establishing a link with the figurative tradition of Western Europe.

In *La Légende du Pauvre Bossu*, the sequence of the narrative unfolds in fixed registers, maintained in a stillness typical of its organisation in separate frames like those that distinguished medieval cycles, and fitting the stylistic choices that were made regarding the setting and the characters. The overall look of the short brings to mind medieval wood engraving with its stylised and two-dimensional images, and it echoes the typical schemes of the visual imagery of the Western European Middle Ages. The entire aesthetic of the movie is inspired by late Middle Ages figurative art, a particularly significant time in the French History of Art. These formal solutions follow in the footsteps of *Les 3 Inventeurs*, characterised by the accurate evocation of the eighteenth century's cultural climate. Ocelot's passion for the history of his country is also evident in this work (Figure 1.8).

The story is about a young hunchback who tries to reach a beautiful princess to win her heart, but he is mistreated and ridiculed by the nobility under the eyes of a laughing crowd.

FIGURE 1.8 *La Légende du Pauvre Bossu*. Ink, charcoal and pastel on paper, 1982. © Ocelot-Studio O / Photo Credit: Denis Vidalie.

After being stabbed in the back, he transforms into an angel and carries the princess with him towards heaven. Budget constraints were again an issue. Consequently, the animation is very scanty, but Ocelot managed to exploit this shortcoming to his advantage. It is the positive characters who move the most, while the negative figures tend to remain stuck in the fixity of the background, as if unable to move and paralysed by their own wickedness and ignorance. The progression of the narration also creates an ascending parabola culminating in the final climax, underlined by the animation that becomes considerably more dynamic in the film's closing moments. In particular, the movements become much more complex and dramatic after the transformation of the protagonist into an angel, and they shift from cutout to traditional cel animation. In fact, the story was born from the director's intention to create a lyrical animation of wings. While looking for inspiration for a new subject, the filmmaker saw some photos of an eagle in flight in a book displaying Muybridge's photographic experiments. Thinking of an animation that included wing beats, he arrived at the final draft of the script: An angel and its opposite, a metamorphosis that would create a well-grounded but equally poetic story. The short film has a great visual impact, very simple and rigorous. It is devoid of dialogues and voice-over, which is an unusual choice for an author who places the story at the centre of his works, but the collaboration with musician Christian Maire continued, and his soundtrack constitutes a superb accompaniment to the development of the plot. The absence of dialogue contributes to creating tension and conveys a dense and compelling atmosphere.

OTHER EARLY PRODUCTIONS

Demonstrating that sometimes one has to wait to reap the fruits of one's labour, the movie *Les 3 Inventeurs* was noticed by the producer Jacqueline Joubert, quite an important figure in French television at the time. From 1977, Joubert was the head of the youth unit of the television channel Antenne 2. She asked Ocelot to write a series for the network and granted him complete creative freedom with regard to the script, the story, the graphics, and the style. The result was the series *La Princesse Insensible* (*The Insensitive Princess*), thirteen episodes of four minutes each, issued in 1984, designed and directed by Ocelot, with the help of a few animators and set to music by the talented Christian Maire. In previous productions, the shorts were made by combining traditional animation and cutouts (Figure 1.9).

In the series *La Princesse Insensible*, all the characters and settings start from delicate and polished graphics which are, in some cases transformed into tiny cut-out figurines or, alternatively, brought to life by means of cel animation. If the drawing style is very different from *Les 3 Inventeurs*, there are many similarities with it in the decorations, both being set in an

FIGURE 1.9 *La Princesse insensible* animation phases. Episode 1: *Le Prince Dompteur.* Ink, watercolour, and coloured adhesive on paper, 1984. © Ocelot – Studio O.

imaginary eighteenth century, allowing the artist to indulge in small details and refined depictions. The mini-series presents some distinctive features. It was commissioned for a children's television show, so Ocelot decided, for the first and last time, to make a movie specifically for children. Nonetheless, he chose not to stage the classic clash between a protagonist and an antagonist but to devote himself to the representation of sheer beauty, enchantment, and delight. *La Princesse Insensible* is a small jewel that reveals a little spark of wonder in each episode.

The princess is indifferent to any solicitation of feelings whatsoever and seems to feel no emotion in the face of anything. For this reason, a competition is held to try to break her coldness in exchange for her hand in marriage. Numerous princes come to her theatre every night to perform a different extraordinary show. This narrative device enables the author to always put on a new and wonderful spectacle, transforming the series into a metaphor for the animated image itself. The princes, just like the filmmaker, have exceptional talents and offer presentations that surprise and astound us. This is analogous to the author's own sorcerer's ability to amaze and make magic, to make gifts to those who are watching, as he often relates when referring to his work in interviews.[24]

A film that is rather at odds with the Ocelot's stylistic creations of those years is the short *Les quatre Vœux* (*The Four Wishes*), a traditional animation made in 1987, using tracing paper with the help of animator Gilles Burgard. The story is based on a fourteenth-century fable, transformed into an entertaining and outrageous script. Villain is a peasant fervently devoted to Saint Martin. Touched by his daily, ardent prayers, the Saint appears to the peasant and offers him four wishes. Villain tells his hefty, disbelieving wife, who laughingly wishes for anatomical changes in her partner's body and Villain replies by expressing the same wish. Saint Martin complies, but eventually, the two are left with less than they started out with. After fulfilling their final, inevitable wish, Saint Martin sighs and departs for Heaven, without sparing a last word of advice first.

The film is very different from the detailed and polished works the author produced for a good part of his career. It is a traditional cel animation achieved with simple, ill-defined, dark strokes on a light background, very little use of colour, and a strongly caricatured outline. It was much appreciated by the public for its ironic vein and the vaguely sexual content of the screenplay and was well-received by the critics. The antiheroine aroused quite a lot of interest as she was far from the delightful and beautiful princesses to which the audience was accustomed at the time. The three characters are extremely well portrayed despite the simplicity of the ensemble, the laughably miserable peasant, the corpulent woman with exaggerated features, and the impassive figure of Saint Martin. Although the movie was chosen for the official selection in the Short Film category at Cannes Festival the same year, the artist considered it to be just a mere divertissement. It can be said that this film was something of a revelation for him. Traditional animation was a long and very monotonous job, "thousands of drawings that are always a bit the same".[25] It was just a brief deviation from the main path he was soon to follow: Silhouette animation.

NOTES

1. *Michel Ocelot en Afrique.* Interview by Juliette Binoche on 3 May 2021, during the third edition of the Branche & Ciné festival, organised by the Office National des Forêts.
2. Ben Nun, Yaël et al. *Michel Ocelot: Artificier de l'imaginaire.* Cinisello Balsamo: Silvana, 2021. Catalogue of the Exhibition at the Musée-Château in Annecy, 2021, p. 11.
3. *Michel Ocelot: De l'ombre à la lumiere.* Interview by Laurent Valière and Stéphane Landfried on the occasion of the 73rd Congrès Dauville 2018: *Hommage à Michel Ocelot*, p. 26.
4. *Portrait de Michel Ocelot.* Documentary by Véronique Martin, France, 2006.
5. *Michel Ocelot: Enchanteur de l'animation à la française.* Interview by Robin Gatto on 5 June 2001.
6. Ben Nun, Yaël et al, *op. cit.*, p. 17.
7. *Le Pharaon, le Sauvage et la Princesse.* Interview by Alexis Clément on Tuesday, 14 June, during the Festival International du Film d'Animation d'Annecy, 2022.
8. Interview included in the DVD *Les Trésors Cachés de Michel Ocelot.* Nord-Ouest, Studio O, France, 2008.
9. *La Belle Epoque de Michel Ocelot.* Documentary by Théo Caillat and Charles Murat, Studio Basho, France, 2020.
10. Chanan, Michael. *Economic Conditions of Early Cinema* in Elsaesser, Thomas. *Early Cinema: Space, Frame, Narrative.* London: British Film Institute, 1990, p. 175.
11. Denis, Sébastien. *Le cinéma d'animation.* Paris: Armand Colin, 2011, p. 225.
12. *Ibid.*, p. 35.
13. Ben Nun, Yaël et al, *op. cit.*, p. 17.
14. Pilling, Jayne. *Animation: 2D and beyond.* New York: RotoVision, 2001, p. 101.

15. Michel Ocelot's official website.
16. Stam, Robert. *Reflexivity in Film and Literature: From Don Quixote to Jean-Luc Godard*. New York: Columbia University Press, 1992, p. XXI.
17. Ben Nun, Yaël et al, *op. cit.*, p. 24.
18. Gautier, Théophile. *Poésies Complètes*. Lost Leaf Publications, 2014, p. 89.
19. Interview by Giannalberto Bendazzi on the occasion of the 11th edition of AniFest, Teplice, Czech Republic, April 26 - May 1, 2012.
20. The stiacciato is a sculptural technique that permits to create a relief or recessed sculpture with carving only millimetres deep. In order to provide the viewer with an illusion of depth, the thickness gradually decreases from the foreground to the background.
21. Personal communication with Michel Ocelot, 25 March 2023.
22. Ibid.
23. Tomasovic, Dick. *Le corps en abîme: Sur la figurine et le cinéma d'animation*. Pertuis: Rouge Profond, 2006, p. 38.
24. Lussier, Marc-André. *Les contes de la nuit: Le sorcier fait son cinéma*. Published 3 March 2012, in *La Presse*, Anjou: La Presse.
25. *Portrait de Michel Ocelot*. Documentary by Véronique Martin, France, 2006.

CHAPTER 2

Silhouette Films

A Magical Night Where Anything Can Happen

THE ADVENTURE OF *CINÉ SI* AND THE COMMITMENT TO THE *PAPIER DÉCOUPÉ*

Some of the distinctive features of Michel Ocelot's filmmaking, already evident in his early works as a director, such as dedication to the re-adaptation of traditional fairy tales and the refinement of the *papier découpé* technique, came to a crucial point with the series *Cine Sì*, creating a total harmony of form and content. *Cine Sì* was a television series broadcast on Canal+ and distributed in English as *Cinema If* and *We are the Star*. Through his friendship with Jean-François Laguionie, the animator could use La Fabrique space and the same old equipment again, to design and shoot the series. Created over the course of two years, the production started in 1987 and the first episode was released in April 1989. The show was initially planned to consist of twenty short films of around twelve minutes. Nevertheless, poor commercial success forced the series to reduce the final number of episodes produced to eight. On the other hand, it attracted much critical acclaim at international festivals and various prizes, including the International Film Critics Award at Annecy Festival, in France, and Best TV series

DOI: 10.1201/9781003292173-3

episode with *Prince et Princess (Prince and Princess)* at the Animated Film Festival in Ottawa, Canada. Most of the work was done in the summer, immersed in nature in the cosy and serene location of La Fabrique, while the post-production was conducted during the intervening winter, in Paris, making this activity particularly enjoyable for the crew, which consisted of only seven members. Similar to how he had managed the production of *Gédéon*, Ocelot chose not to subdivide the work, but to entrust each of the animators with an episode while he personally took care of the concept, screenplay, and direction. As a matter of fact, as pointed out by Pierre Jouvanceau, "the very existence of the genre" of silhouette animation is "essentially tied to the work of lone animators",[1] accompanied by extremely small crews even in the case of serial or feature productions. This characteristic massively affects the production, which tends to be slower, in addition to centralising much of the creative process in the hands of the director. Silhouette-animated cinema is not conducive to the specialisation of tasks. Rather, it is the director who mostly brings together functions that would normally be entrusted to professionals specialising in specific areas such as drawing, colouring, actual animation, and so on.

This work method, derived from the animation genre, was exploited to the fullest by Ocelot, resulting in a high level of quality, a degree of variety, and richness of craftsmanship absent in serial productions, which were flattened by homogenised standardisation.[2] As recounted by Georges Sifianos, Ocelot's collaborator at the time, the enormous freedom granted by both the direction and the venue allowed them to work at their own pace, sometimes even preferring night to day, according to the inspiration of the moment, or to take advantage of the nocturnal calm that best suited the work approaches some of the anima-tors. Such a privileged working context allowed the collaborators to experiment and benefit from considerable creative freedom while enjoying the delights of country life: Taking a walk to the nearby waterfall where one could bathe; spending time calmly observing insects and small reptiles; establishing a daily tea ceremony involving the director and the entire crew.[3]

In July 1988 Bénédicte Galup joined the animation équipe, and she would go on to become a key collaborator in the following years. Galup was fresh out of Beaux-Arts in Montpellier and became part of the crew to help the animators with all sorts of tasks, such as preparing the various puppets or sets. "I had only a basic knowledge of animation. Like a master with his apprentice, Michel completed, step by step, my training in this job with patience and passion," she recounted.[4] Galup, from the initial role of all-hands, gradually progressed to more-specific tasks, helping with the animation for the episode *Le Garçon des Figues* (*The Fig Boy*) in the summer of 1988, whereas in the summer of 1989, she animated the entire episode entitled *On ne saurait penser à tout* (*One can't think of everything*). The crew worked with 16 mm cameras and silver film, which Ocelot had learned to use to the fullest from his previous experiences. Galup recalled the process involved:

> To create the special effects, the film was repeatedly passed in front of the lens to be more or less "burned out". We juggled with covers and countercovers, with the diaphragm and camera lenses, with filters, etc. [...] All this without the possibility to check our work (as is constantly done in computer graphics today) before the rolls came back from the lab. Each take was a challenge that required great concentration and, above all, the need not to be overwhelmed by the fear of failure.[5]

The series was conceived by combining the dual need to produce a marketable material without renouncing artistic ambitions. Hence, Ocelot created a structure that well suited the conception of completely independent stories. Each short is preceded by a prologue: A girl and a boy meet every night in a disused movie theatre to stage wonderful stories that transport them across centuries and let them cross country borders. They choose the characters they would like to play, and they design the costumes, music, and settings, with the help of an expert projectionist. The recurrence of the same characters gives continuity to the show, while allowing the episodes to be set in completely different times and places, some of these in specific countries and bygone eras, while one of them, designed in a retro-futuristic style, is set in an unspecified time in the future. With few means at his disposal, the author decided to focus on the simplicity and effectiveness of a technique he had already begun to master, cut-out animation. In this case, the author preferred to use black silhouettes, with a backlit coloured background, even more essential than white figurines, and directly borrowed from Lotte Reiniger's early films. The French filmmaker acknowledged the debt and influence of the great pioneer of silhouette cinema,[6] and on the other hand he repeatedly emphasised how her style and animation were not to his particular liking.[7] Nonetheless, he drew as much from her figurative repertoire as from her aptitude for fable storytelling. Undoubtedly, merit is due to Ocelot for having revived a nearly forgotten genre of animation, recalling "the days of magic lanterns and Chinese shadow silhouettes",[8] modernising it and making it accessible to a wide audience through excellent stylistic and aesthetic renovation (Figure 2.1).

The process of renewal of the figurative language was similar to the operation carried out on the structure of classical narration. Ocelot wittily stretched the definition of the fairy tale, aware of handling material based on an established tradition and pliable, to be reworked and transformed at will. With this metaphor, he summed up his work:

> I use everyone's ideas in my own way. I play with balls that countless jugglers have used from century to century. These balls, which have been passed from hand to hand, are not new. But today I am the one juggling.[9]

FIGURE 2.1 *La Princesse des Diamants.* Articulated paper marionettes on scenery. Black paper cut-outs and watercolour on paper, 1989. © Ocelot-Studio O.

Such was always his approach to the structure of tales, convinced that there are no completely new ideas, but only reinterpretations of what we have assimilated by reading or watching already existing creations. This awareness places Ocelot on a privileged plane with respect to the reworking of stories. Showing the viewers visual sources and making citationism a real stylistic mark, thus becomes a method of involving the spectator in the creation of meaning. The reworking of stories is shown as a collective process, as already theorised by Roland Barthes in his essay "The Death of the Author", in which the text is defined as "a multi-dimensional space in which a variety of writings, none of them original, blend and clash. The text is a tissue of quotations drawn from the innumerable centres of culture".[10]

The filmmaker chose to expose his artifice, therefore the prologue to the shorts not only fulfils a connecting role but in addition to creating continuity and affection for the characters on the part of the audience, it becomes a "bracketing narrative device" revealing that these films are "about representation, narration, and animation".[11] Self-reflexive style in *Les 3 Inventeurs* already had assumed a fundamental role by foregrounding the relationship between material and fiction, an ingenious idea engendered by the need to circumvent difficulties of creating an animated story with a tight budget. As noted by Richad Neupert, with *Cine Si* the same practical necessity was overcome by exploiting a frames-within-frames device, a *mise en abyme* capable of multiplying fictional levels, metaphor, and reflection on the role of the artist. As the protagonists stage their own invented stories, further handcrafting their own costumes and scenarios, "the production ends up justifying perfectly its own eccentric, home-made look"[12] and reflecting on cinematic fiction itself.

Equally, the appropriation of tales by the characters, who enjoy creating variations of traditional fables – and the particular attention given to the performative act of presenting the story to the audience – reconnects Ocelot's work to the oral tradition,[13] a theme particularly dear to the director and one that would be openly remarked upon in his filmography by the introduction of certain figures, as the Griotte in the film *Kirikou et les Hommes et les Femmes*. Unveiling the creative process was an overt objective. The two protagonists and their assistants show us the research work among the most disparate figurative sources that the author himself carries out when creating a story. Ocelot involves us in his own painstaking studies of the figurative heritage of other cultures, led by the desire to create from

FIGURE 2.2 *La Manteau de la Vieille Dame*. Black paper cut-outs and watercolour on paper, 1989. The scene is based on a print by Japanese artist Katsushika Hokusai, *The Hanging-Cloud Bridge at Mount Gyōdō near Ashikaga*. © Ocelot-Studio O.

accurate documentation, as is the case with the Hokusai prints shown to the viewer before incorporating them into the story set in Japan: *Le Manteau de la Vieille Dame* (*The Old Lady's Coat*) (Figure 2.2).

In turn, Ocelot reveals his fervent passion for art, graphic design, theatre, and performance. He opens the audience up to the possibilities of playing with imagination "and perhaps give people ideas and push them to invent and activate".[14] He also emphasises the transformative power of stories. Manipulating traditional fairy tales, or telling new ones – as the characters do in the prologue of each episode – prompts us to read reality through a more conscious gaze.

In 1992, the eight episodes created for *Cine Si* were complemented by three other shorts brought together under the name of *Les Contes de la Nuit* (*Tales of the Night*), created with the same technique and willingness to reimagine the narrative patterns of the fairy tale. The short movies are varied in terms of plot and settings, yet they are unified by the edifying tone as well as by dynamics openly in opposition to the norms dictated by tradition. In the late 1980s and early 1990s, dedicating oneself to the creation of an animated fairy tale movie in France, meant challenging the hegemonic Disney canon and its conservative ideology, but also inscribing the film in a rather well-established tradition of artistic experimentation, in the footsteps of other animators such as Paul Grimault and Laguionie – a path that afterwards would be brilliantly carried on by Florence Miailhe. The works of these directors, animated in a particular painterly style, already displayed a shift away from traditional roles, a characteristic feature of both French live-action and animated cinema from the postwar period onward.[15] Questioning the conventions of traditional narratives meant calling into question also the societal structures that produced them, and Ocelot chose to do so through the inclusion of metanarrative devices that create both a direct relationship with reality and a space of overt fiction. The filmmaker stated, "My fairy tales are not stories to escape, but to open our eyes to real things. In fact, in my films I advertise reality".[16] In this regard, the sharp separation between reality and fiction plays a crucial part and is emphasised by keeping alive the relationship with the theatrical element of staging: The owl acting as a clapperboard, in the two series of *Cine Sì* and *Les Contes de la Nuit*, the opening of a curtain in both *Les 3 Inventeurs* and *La Princesse Insensible*. By rewriting the stories we all know, Ocelot prompts us to think that anyone can contribute to imagining a different reality.

Two themes recur most frequently in each of the stories: The exaltation of kindness and nobility of spirit, which triumphs over arrogance and power; the questioning of traditional and rigid gender roles. These two elements often intersect, as "usually the losing force is strongly marked as overly confident and patriarchal",[17] Positive figures emerge because of their intelligence and humility, such as the young man who, in *La Princesse des Diamants* (*The Diamond Princess*), succeeds in winning the challenge, aided by the ants who had benefited from his kindness. The tale features a princess trapped and immobilised by a spell, which can be broken by a prince able to find the one hundred and eleven diamonds needed to reassemble her necklace. Where the first suitor, swaggering and contemptuous, fails, the second one, endowed with courage and goodness of heart, triumphs, thanks to the help of ants who were none other than former pretenders transformed by the same maleficent spell. Similarly, in the two shorts *La Sorcière* (*The Witch*) and *La Reine Cruelle et le Montreur de Fabulo* (*The Cruel Queen and the Fabulo Trainer*), the young male protagonists manage to find the key to dialogue with two seemingly cruel and frightening female characters. *La Sorcière* depicts an impenetrable and indestructible castle, which a boy is able to enter simply by asking permission, only to discover that the witch who inhabits it, painted by all as ruthless, is none other than a brilliant and kind-hearted inventor. The character of the witch, besides being an unconventional female figure, is a self-representation, as stated by the author himself.[18] Her castle is in fact a creative forge, bewitching the viewer with countless fantastic scenarios and strange contraptions. While everyone was trying to destroy the castle in order to win the princess's hand, the protagonist manages to enter it and finally chooses to stand by the witch and live with her, breaking with the predictability of the traditional ending. In *La Reine Cruelle et le Montreur de Fabulo*, the humble Fabulo trainer uses his inventive skills and humility to understand the queen's needs while music becomes a common language that manages to give emotion to the fearsome ruler. In both cases, emphasis is placed on generosity and kindness, combined with the celebration of creative and imaginative qualities.

Regarding gender roles, these are often altered by primarily proposing female characters differing from the narrative norms of fairy tales, where characters are delineated as stereotypical figures intended to reinforce "the patriarchal symbolical order based on rigid notions of sexuality and gender."[19] As pointed out by Yaël Ben Nun:

> By hijacking the codes of representation of princes and princesses, Michel Ocelot touches on the issue of gender representation and invites us to question the social models and values conveyed by traditional fairy tales. His princesses often have nothing to envy their male partners, neither the intelligence nor the ability to act.[20]

Nonetheless, in many cases, women in positions of power, such as the cruel queen or the pharaohess, are characterised as negative and overbearing figures. This choice can likewise be interpreted as a critique of the corruptive nature of power, to bring out the contrast with the other humble and naive characters, and thus lends itself to different and nuanced interpretations. It remains, though, a repurposing of a literary topos that would also be reproduced in other later films. Among the female figures who most emerge as positive, innovative and captivating, there certainly is the aforementioned witch, an intelligent, creative woman, a female model beyond the norm of classical narrative. Moreover, it should be highlighted that the figure of the princess in *La Princesse des Diamants,* who, despite her immobility and her role as a princess to be rescued, is shown to be purposeful and resolute.

In some of the shorts, the classic binary and romantic relationship between man and woman is still in order. However, an overt willingness to break these boundaries is evident, moreover, in clear advance of the Disney fairy tales offered on the screens in that period and in subsequent years. The films that challenge gender roles most of all are the 1989 Cine Sì episode *Prince et Princesse (Prince and Princess)* and the 1992 short *Bergère qui danse (The Dancing Shepherdess).* The latter is a sort of overturned rewriting of Sleeping Beauty's story, in which a total reversal of roles is displayed, as it is the girl who saves the boy, thanks to her skills as a dancer and not the other way around. In *Prince et Princesse,* a prince and a princess share their first kiss, which begins a series of amusing transformations sparked by every other kiss: The two involuntarily turn into toads, whales, snails, giraffes, butterflies, and other animals, ending when the princess and prince find themselves in each other's bodies. The result is that the girl will be allowed to perform typically male activities, while the prince will have to readjust to the role of the princess, who waits for her beloved by embroidering while he is on the hunt. A clever and surprising ending aimed at stimulating the viewer to reflect, although it should be pointed out that this last exchange subverts gender roles but does not undermine the rigidity of the heteronormative couple. It is worth mentioning this aspect since, as pointed out in the book *Animating Difference: Race, Gender, and Sexuality in Contemporary Films for Children,*[21] the vast majority of traditional cartoons apply a heterosexist lens. The authors remarked how characters in animated films are perceived to have no sexuality since heterosexual sexuality is generally considered the norm. Thus, given the normativity of heterosexuality, its constant representations often go unnoticed. However, if animation can be considered, like any other cultural expression, as a vehicle for transmitting valuable lessons, it is worth emphasising the role that heterosexual romance can play as a device for maintaining the status quo.

OCELOT AND THE HISTORY OF SILHOUETTE ANIMATION

The history of animated silhouette cinema does not begin with Lotte Reiniger, yet she can be considered the pioneer of this genre and the filmmaker who made it recognised and appreciated around the world. Reiniger is best known for her 1926 feature film *Die Abenteuer des Prinzen Achmed* (*The Adventures of Prince Achmed*), one of the very first animated features in history and the oldest still preserved today. Obsessed with cut-out silhouettes from an early age, the artist tried her hand not only at animated films but also at shadow theatre, from which tradition she drew many cues for her creations. Throughout the course of her career, she continued to use animated silhouette technique to bring her characters to life, and in the last years of her life, with enormous generosity, she expended her energy ensuring that this genre would be known and understood, leaving us a considerable body of writings and videos in which she recounted the secrets of manipulating her cardboard puppets. The animated image was a means for the pioneer to make fantastic stories come to life; indeed, the medium lent itself to the representation of the many surprising metamorphoses described in fairy tales. Reiniger's genius led her to conceive a feature-length animated film with an extremely complex technique. The silhouettes posed many challenges, which she and her team of experienced anima-tors tackled by finding many innovative solutions, including an early form of the multiplane camera, subsequently adopted, im-proved, and patented by Walt Disney. The result was extremely rich films, both technically and stylistically, accordant with the hyperdecoratism and descriptive opulence typical of 1920s ex-pressionist cinema.

The production of *Prince Achmed* stimulated many authors to venture into silhouette cinema, generating numerous epigones as well as true masters in Europe and abroad, among whom the most significant are Tony Sarg, who worked mainly in North America; Japanese animator Noburo Ofuji, and versatile German animator Bruno J. Böttge. The seemingly limited expressive possibilities of the medium were expanded by the animators, according to their own style or to the tastes of the time. As ex-plained by Pierre Jouvanceau in his book *The Silhouette Film*, it's possible to divide them into two main currents: A so-called baroque line and a minimalist line, as well as a third way that mixes the two trends, often achieving less convincing effects.[22] Reiniger remained, however, the one and only real point of reference when the French author chose the black silhouettes in

1987, as the circulation of animated silhouette films was always rather sparse. Ocelot was fascinated by the expressive power of this genre; nonetheless, he chose to purge it of the extremely elaborate style employed by Reiniger and turned towards a simplification of the form, favouring clarity and rejecting the baroque and elaborate sophistication of her expressionist cinema. Cropping silhouettes was not new to the French director, yet the substitution of white for black multiplied the limitations, as this colour cancelled out any formal indication, allowing only a global identification of the subject represented. The technique employed was the same as Reiniger's – except for the exclusive use of cardboard, where the German filmmaker sometimes preferred to utilise thin lead sheets – with some minor modifications, one of the most significant being the cropping of the eye in the heads of the cut-out puppets. The system of small gears already employed in the making of *Les 3 Inventeurs* was retained and complemented by other expedients and practical solutions to make the work in the animation stages as easy as possible. Ocelot's methodological approach also differed from Reiniger's in the construction stages of the figurines. Both started with preparatory drawings. However, where the German filmmaker went from drawing directly to cutting out the silhouettes, the French artist developed a more articulated system. Ocelot created models that would then serve as a reference for the later creation of his puppets[23] (Figure 2.3).

Moreover, when necessary, other techniques were combined with the cutout, such as cel animation for defining some clothing details or realising the sparkling jewellery; or in the case of the mega-radar in *La Reine Cruelle et le Montreur de Fabulo*, created using the bottom of a soda bottle animated in stop motion.[24] Achieving the desired effect very often meant blending different techniques, as was also the case in *Le Manteau de la Vieille Dame*. Set in Hokusai's Japan, the short tells the story of an encounter between an elderly lady, adorable and fond of poetry, and a criminal, intent on stealing her coat. Anticipating his

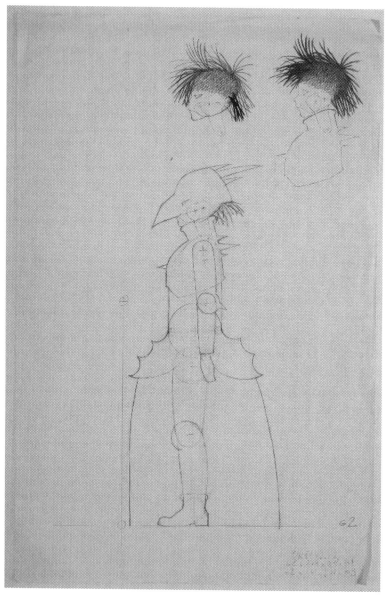

FIGURE 2.3   *La Sorcière.* Model sheet, pencil on tracing paper, 1989.
© Ocelot-Studio O / Photo Credit: Denis Vidalie.

actions, the old lady mounts the back of the man, leading him through bumpy roads full of obstacles on a journey across the country. In order to preserve the complexity of their movements, these were drawn frame by frame, as in the classic cartoon. The drawings were then combined with the two superimposed figurines, the old lady and the young man, without altering the final result: Black, graceful, minimalistic silhouettes.[25]

Having established that Ocelot's work can be characterised as a distinctly minimalist style, his research was oriented towards an elegant and idealised aesthetic rather than realism, although without compromising the understanding of what the audience sees on the screen. Conversely, in some of the more baroque works, including some scenes from Lotte Reiniger's films, the excessive stylistic embellishment contributed to confusing the viewer and did not allow them to easily distinguish the outlines of the figures. Ocelot, therefore, exploited the evocative power of stylised forms by placing emphasis on the definition of contours, the exactness of cropped details, and the legibility of scenes. The backgrounds and settings are played on the prevalence of voids over full-on compositions 'set on solid, well-thought-out geometries; the figures – with faces in profile, an almost mandatory choice in this genre of cinema – are outlined by a few fairly simple features. This did not mean renouncing more decoratively elaborate and finely crafted scenery; in fact, great attention was paid to the study of decorative and ornamental elements in both costumes and settings, as in the case of the structure enclosing the princess in *La Princesse des Diamants*, inspired by the graceful forms of Parisian Art Nouveau architecture, in the interiors of the Gothic witch's castle, and in the description of the princesses' dresses. However, the aesthetic research, rather than verisimilitude, is directed to a more exact characterisation of the figures. Such an intention can be discerned in *La Reine Cruelle et le Montreur de Fabulo*: The retro-futuristic style is accentuated by the geometrisation of forms in order to amplify the lines chosen for the definition of the queen's

FIGURE 2.4 *La Reine Cruelle et le Montreur de Fabulo*. Articulated paper marionette on scenery. Black paper cutouts and watercolour on paper, 1989. © Ocelot-Studio O.

clothes and features, played on pointed shapes and acute angles, aimed at specifying the harshness and rigidity of her temperament (Figure 2.4).

The same role is reserved for the use of close-ups. In nearly all silhouette cinema, close-ups are rather rare and always limited to "the role of enlargement, never to the expression of affect",[26] but since Ocelot's main purpose is to maintain a rather strong connection with reality, the close-up has a primarily expressive function. A large part of the close-ups is reserved for faces, revealing more closely some of the expedients, capable of partly eluding the vagueness of the black paper. Such shots were obtained, as in Reninger's cinema, by exclusively constructing the body parts needed in larger dimensions: The head, the neck, and the upper torso. One of the most effective innovations devised by Ocelot is the choice of cropping the outline of the eyes in black

FIGURE 2.5 *Le Garçon des Figues.* Articulated paper marionette on scenery. Black paper cut-outs and watercolour on paper, 1989. Musée-Château d'Annecy collection.

cardboard, ensuring quite a wide range of expressive possibilities for the characters. Therefore, facial expressions could be shown through the movements and angles of the eyes, especially when framed at close range. Similarly, the mouths and jaws are mobile, signalling with some accuracy the characters' feelings and emotions[27] (Figure 2.5).

The renewal of expressive language was also reflected in Ocelot's handling of animation. One of the criticisms most often brought to cut-out animation concerned the lack of fluidity of movement, a judgment that suffered from the heavy cultural weight of animated drawing, considered for decades to be the dominant model to follow and compare with.[28] The silhouettes were accused of being a handcrafted, naïve product, and the animation jerky and poorly engaging; some went so far as to call them "hopping grasshoppers".[29] Such a criticism, negatively conditioned by the cultural hegemony of the cartoon, was in part rooted, however, in a certain style of animation that many tended to follow: Reiniger herself recommended a preference for faster, more concise movements to infuse the figures with expressiveness and to obviate the possible monotony derived from technical limitations. Nonetheless, it would be wrong to believe that cut-out animation can exclusively operate within the framework of exaggerated and extremely rapid movement. As noted by Pierre Jouvenceau,[30] Ocelot preferred calm rhythm and measured movements, practising a purification of gesture that echoes the sobriety of the scenarios and the simplification of the scripts. The characters, rather than by their outward appearance, are primarily defined by their behaviours and actions, although the animation does not accentuate the intentions of the figurines with the excessive motility typical of other authors, such as Tony Sarg and, to a lesser extent, Lotte Reiniger. Animation features are reverberated in the rare and smooth camera movements, in addition to the simplification of narrative space, oriented towards two-dimensionality rather than the layering of volumes sought in the works of other authors. Ocelot used some over-lapping glass to create a focus and out-of-focus effect to generate a sense of greater depth, as in the case of the Japanese fable, where the figures in the foreground and background with respect to the protagonists are blurred to create a wide depth-of-field effect.[31] Nonetheless, these devices are not comparable to those implemented by Reiniger with her multiplane camera.

Simplicity would remain a constant also in his later silhouette films, where Ocelot's style does not change, despite the renewed possibilities given by digital animation. Ocelot organises the space into two non-communicating planes: The background, consisting of the coloured backdrop and eventual architecture, and the foreground, reserved for the black silhouettes. The figures also always stand on a ground plane, whereas in Reininger's films they tend to float, to give a greater impression of movement. His stylistic choices strongly differ from Reiniger's, as well as from other artists, even coeval ones, as in the case of David Anderson's 1982 short *Dreamland Express,* a silhouette animated short that employed very pronounced perspective patterns and focusing devices to obtain a greater impression of depth. The same argument can be brought for later series produced with computer graphics. Ocelot's choice again falls on formal cleanliness, by rarely creating any coherent depth or volume cues. A disposition to draw on figurative two-dimensional figurative art powerfully emerges, even in the presence of other viable alternatives. When the French author would re-approach silhouettes, the film *The Mysterious Geographic Explorations of Jasper Morello* (Anthony Lucas, 2005) had recently been issued, a diametrically opposed example to the French director's works. In *The Mysterious Geographic Explorations of Jasper Morello,* despite the predilection for 2D animation with only marginal intervention of digital, the depth effects reach high levels of sophistication. Lucas' work revolves around the search for complexity and depth of cinematic space, whereas Ocelot prefers to obliterate narrative space in favour of clarity and readability.

If, from the figurative point of view, Ocelot can rightly be placed within the minimalist line, the same cannot be said for his extensive and accurate use of sound effects, which led his films to acquire a strong quality of verisimilitude. Silhouette animation was born as sound cinema – Lotte Reiniger envisioned a musical part-script, completed before the filming and timed to fit the scenes to the musical rhythms. Many animators would follow her example, including the French filmmaker, who gave a privileged role to sound and soundtrack in all his films and would often record the dialogue before making the animations. A large part of the enthralling power of his early silhouette films is due to the outstanding contribution of Christian Maire, newly entrusted to compose the soundtrack. The musician mixed baroque and nineteenth-century musical instruments with electronic keyboards and synthesisers, achieving extremely evocative and enchanting results. In particular, some moments remain etched in the mind thanks to the music, capable of expanding the sense of wonder: The concussive and hypnotic rhythms accompanying the hectic search for diamonds; the musical accompaniment with cello during the exploration of the witch's castle and the unforgettable melodious song of the Fabulo.

Additionally, Ocelot was the first to dub the silhouettes in order to make the characters converse. Direct dialogues had never been used before he did it, bringing a real transformation within the genre, as the sound would help to reinforce the characterisation of the figures, emphasising their moral attributes and establishing a deeper relationship with the viewer. Following the theories of Etienne Souriau, Richard Neupert argued that much of the credibility of the characters in Ocelot's movies, in addition to movement, is due to the sound accompaniment, which can "help further exercise a strong physical sensation on the viewer."[32] The director exploited the multisensory suggestion of diegetic sounds to give body to the flat figurines and help the audience with the process of understanding and bonding with the cinematic character, as sound is strongly interrelated to the perception of them as embodied. This is especially relevant as the stories put on stage are fantastical and fabulous, but closely anchored in reality.

The relationship established between characters and audience is, furthermore, fundamental, since the filmmaker has among his main purposes the transmission of edifying messages, following the grammar of the traditional fairy tale. In this regard, Ocelot's animations are antithetical to films where silhouettes are used with deliberately depersonalising intent, as in the case of the artistic productions of Kara Walker and William Kentdrige. In Walker's work, in particular, a different relationship to the culture that originally produced the art of silhouettes is discernible. For Walker, it is crucial to generate a contrast between form and content; in fact, the silhouettes are symbolic of the same colonialist culture that produced racism and brutality, the main themes of her work. Walker's silhouettes are used to emphasise the stereotyping of racialised people, and in her films, the figures are animated as live puppets and filmed, as in the case of the 2007 film ... *calling to me from the angry surface of some grey and threatening sea. I was transported.* Leaving aside the inherent symbolic significance of direct puppet animation in relation to the issue of slavery, depersonalisation is achieved through a number of technical devices. The absence of dubbing contributes to the silence of the characters. Unlike Ocelot's, Walker figures are significantly reduced to beings lacking any psychological depth, contributing to sharply distancing their experience from that of the viewer and creating an effect of estrangement. The French director's intentions are the opposite; he employs silhouettes without particular signification and associates them with a traditional narrative form such as the fairy tale, creating a harmonious result that avoids any effect of disaffection and unpleasantness. He strives for a strong identification of the audience with the character, managing to achieve the objective through numerous devices, from sound to dubbing, from stylistic choices to animation. The depiction of conflicts is simplified and schematised, in part by softening it in order for the message to pass smoothly and reach a wide and varied audience, to have a beneficial impact on the viewers, spontaneously inviting them to reflection.

THE RETURN OF THE SILHOUETTE FAIRYTALES: *DRAGONS ET PRINCESSES*

In 2010, the director had the opportunity to return to the short story format of his early days and bring to life some of the tales he had elaborated upon more than twenty years earlier. The format not only responded to commercial needs but also met the filmmaker's desire to develop both short and long stories.

> I like all formats. I work in many formats and on many types of project, with no limitation beyond my own desire to tell stories and illustrate them. Yet some of my

greatest emotional responses as a spectator have come from short films seen at animation festivals. Because the animated short films that I enjoy come from the guts of half-crazed individuals like me, who know they'll never get rich from their productions, which will be seen by relatively few people. They work without compromise, and with no pressure other than that of their imperious need to create.[33]

The TV series *Dragons et Princesses* (*Dragons and Princesses*) was composed of ten short stories of thirteen minutes, created in seventeen months using the technique of black silhouette on a coloured background. With several feature films under his belt and a completely different budget, Ocelot chose to return to the enchanting genre of shadow theatre, "a magical night where anything can happen".[34]

The series was first broadcast in October 2010, produced by Nord-Ouest Films in co-production with Canal+ and Studio O, the production company founded by Ocelot in 1992. The silhouettes were designed after a hand-drawn model, then animated exclusively with digital tools, but following the same criteria used more than two decades earlier. Ocelot created the models, then brought the paper puppets and showed the computer professionals what to do. Each episode was conceived, written and directed by him, while the implementation phases were entrusted to restricted creative groups of just a few collaborators. The crew was composed of seventeen multi-skilled computer graphics artists, some of whom met during the production of *Azur & Asmar*.

The use of computerised imaging did not affect the style already established in the past, and retained the same enchantment as the earlier shorts, with additional richness provided by the shimmering sets. The shorts are constructed exactly as in *Ciné Si*, with the same prologue during which the stories are discussed, the sources cleverly shown to the audience, and the creative process highlighted. The narrative and aesthetic style maintained the simplicity and synthesis already experienced in the past. The filmmaker recounted how telling a story in black silhouettes was sometimes a challenge.[35] In the absence of colour, the space for action remained extremely limited, so he decided to focus on the fineness of details visible in backlighting, and in the precise definition of profiles and clothing. Among the inspirations that guided his work was the art of ancient Egypt, greatly appreciated by the animator for its extreme simplification and clarity. Already at the time of the *Ciné Si* series, *Le Garçon des Figues*, set in Egypt, was counted among the shorts with the most harmonious achievement, since the sparse mise-en-scène blended nicely with the delicately elaborated details while maintaining a firm minimalism. In *Dragons et Princesses*, the sobriety of the old settings was replaced by the magnificence of rutilant computer-generated backgrounds, characterised by flat colours and stark two-dimensional space. However, as in *Azur & Asmar*, the decorative richness of the backdrops did not interfere with the purity of the curves and the essentiality of the outlines. The audacious and original style was combined with a simple and straightforward narrative, a characteristic element of all Ocelot's tales. The scenarios are organised around rigorous and symmetrical structures. More than eight hundred settings appear in the series, inspired by different cultures and historical eras, in which more than three hundred characters take life. The combination of these elegant black silhouettes with intricate architecture and fabulous scenery yielded a powerful image that produced an enduring impression of aesthetic enjoyment (Figure 2.6).

The return to the shadow theatre was no coincidence. One of the most interesting features of the artist's oeuvre is his ability to handle different techniques, experimenting and overcoming the limits of genres and means employed from case to case. Nevertheless, silhouette film would be so crucial that it would also aesthetically orientate works created with other techniques, whether cel animation or CGI. Once again, neither was this

FIGURE 2.6 *Les Contes de la Nuit. La Fille Biche et le Fils de l'Architecte.* CGI animation, 2011. © Nord-Ouest Films / Studio O / StudioCanal.

exactly the same technique practised in the past, nor was it merely an adaptation to new technologies. The experiments and innovations carried out went in the direction of creating something unprecedented, holding true to the statements of a 1991 interview, which foreshadow some of the choices Ocelot would make in later years.

> Ideally, I would change my technique for each film. For me, one of the qualities of animation is that it is both an art and a craft. You design things with your intellect, but at certain moments you have to roll up your sleeves and struggle with the material, find solutions to get by materially [...] Art depends partly on technique, and I like to change my technique to enter – and make others enter – different universes, which cannot be reached otherwise.[36]

Before shooting a film, the filmmaker started with a filmed sketch, a series of still images with his own voice speaking all the roles. Called *animatics*, this procedure allows the crew to get a clear idea of how a film will proceed before it is made. The animation then followed the dialogue that had already been recorded. Christophe Rossignon, the producer, was in the habit of reserving a small role for himself in each film he produced. The director, therefore, thought of giving him a small part, his first-ever animated role. Ocelot's voice can also be heard at some points. When recording the actors' proper voices, he would sometimes choose one of the roles he felt most comfortable with. But usually, he would fill in a line here and there for a missing extra. Musical numbers were composed by Christian Maire, who worked side-by-side with the director and contributed to adding profundity to the tales. Especially effective is the intervention of the choirs in *L'élue de la Ville d'Or* (*The Chosen Girl of the Golden City*). The story tells of an Aztec town condemned to a terrible curse: Four times a year, its inhabitants are obliged to sacrifice the most beautiful girl in the town. Ocelot imagined associating the senseless horror of these sacrifices with the beauty of the choruses, which he envisioned as those in Verdi's opera.[37]

The ten tales are set in locations far apart in time and place. Ocelot had always loved to draw from very different cultures placed in various corners of the globe. This choice had been variously interpreted. Some have read it as a positive sign of cultural consolidation and the externalisation of a "desire for elsewhere".[38] It was also commented on negatively, describing its spirit as "closer to a colonial display than to that of Charles Perrault".[39] It can be argued that the constant reference to figurative sources consulted during the prologues of the shorts suggests a forthright relationship with the culture with which the director is dealing. Thus, the scenery would be a tribute to the artistic heritage of the countries represented and a way to celebrate their cultural richness. However, in the episode *L'élue de la Ville d'Or,* the dialectic between the foreign character and the local population portrays a relation of subordination that harks back to a slightly colonial vision. Indeed, the boy has the role of exposing and destroying the superstitions of the locals, who passively accepted their fate without rebelling or questioning. This tone of vague superiority is also corroborated by a traditionalist view of gender roles, where the young maiden waits helplessly to be sacrificed, standing in the classic role of a woman in distress to be rescued.

Indeed, it should be emphasised how Ocelot's attempts to bridge gender stereotypes in this series are rather timid and not always effective. This is also surprising given the freedom with which Ocelot had treated the narrative material more than two decades earlier. Moreover, this traditionalism cannot be ascribed to mere repetition of folk tales crystallised in time, as the director often remarked on his intervention to modify the stories to his liking and to communicate his messages accurately. Some shorts show quite disruptive characters. Remarkable is the figure of the little girl in *La Maîtresse des Monstres* (*The Monsters' Mistress*), at odds with a conservative narrative. The story tells of a group of people forced to live in the bowels of the earth, terrorised by monstrous creatures that block the exit to the outside world. With the help of a small animal, the little girl, mistreated by everyone up to that point, discovers that she has the strength and power to defeat the frightful beings and finally free herself from captivity. She is described as the only repository of common sense and the sole person able to face the terrible monsters of the cave, and she is an extremely forceful figure especially since she is a child. On the other hand, other female roles are modelled on tradition and stereotypes. The women in *Ti Jean et la Belle-sans-Connaître* (*Ti Jean and the Beauty not Known*) are depicted as completely passive, a mere trophy to be handed over to the victorious hero. *Le Loup-Garou* (*The Werewolf*) tells of two sisters competing for the same boy. When it turns out that he is a werewolf, the two reactions are completely opposite. The tale is outstandingly poetic. Delicate and touching is the relationship between the girl in love and the wolf. Nonetheless, the two sisters respectively embody the stereotype of the ruthless and overbearing woman or the gentle girl who is completely devoted to the man she loves. Love, moreover, heterosexual love, seems to be the young girl's only reason for living.[40]

Furthermore, the relationship between the three characters in the prologue is sometimes asymmetrical, the boy can choose many adventurous and active roles for himself, whereas the girl is often reserved for passive and traditionalist parts; in many cases, she is simply the hero's lover. Her subordination is especially evident in the prologue of the episode *Le Garçon qui ne mentait jamais* (*The Boy who Never Lied*). Initially, the girl refuses to impersonate such a horrible and cruel princess, then she is pushed to give in and lend herself as an actress for the play. In the story, the male protagonist is tested by two kings who bet on his loyalty. The daughter of one of the two rulers helps to deceive the boy and, in an act of profound cruelty, forces him to kill his beloved talking horse. "I could be the boy, but not the horrid princess! Not only can I not identify with her, but also, I would never be able to come up with her criminal duplicity",[41] declared Ocelot. In this regard, it is worth asking whether in this instance the director has sufficiently questioned the possibilities for his female audience, whether children or adults, to identify with various positive characters. In 2011 another short film was shot, which in contrast was based on a particularly felicitous ploy. It was called *La Fille Biche et le Fils de l'Architecte* (*The Doe Girl and the Architect's Son*) and tells the story of a girl who is turned into an animal by a sorcerer when she refuses to marry him, as she is in love with the architect's son. During the course of the story, we believe that the girl has taken on the appearance of a doe, when in fact she has been transformed into a raven. The short film ends with this final little twist that contributes to a less-flattened view of gender roles, avoiding the association between the beautiful helpless girl and the tender fawn.

La Fille Biche et le Fils de l'Architecte was developed to be assembled together with five other stories from the TV series *Dragons et Princesses*, in order to create the feature *Les Contes de la Nuit* (*Tales of the Night* – 2011). The director recounted that when the producers saw the TV series they were amazed at the extraordinary quality of the work and immediately undertook to

FIGURE 2.7 *Dragons et Princesses. Ivan Tsarévitch et la Princesse Changeante.* Digital colour chart, 2010. The graphic motifs are inspired by the work of Russian artist Ivan Bilibine. © Nord-Ouest Films / Studio O / Canal +.

produce a cinema transposition. They also drew from the same series to shape the movie *Ivan Tsarévitch et la Princesse Changeante* (*Ivan Tsarévitch and the Changing Princess* – 2016), consisting of a total of four episodes, none of which were unreleased. Both films were produced by Nord-Ouest, in co-production with StudioCanal and Studio O (Figure 2.7).

These two silhouettes features were modeled after *Princes et Princesses* (*Princes and Princesses*), released in 2000. The movie also consisted of a collection of six short stories from the 1989 *Ciné Si* series. Its production was suggested by the distributor of *Kirikou et la Sorcière*, Marc Bonny, who had seen these unknown shorts and wanted to distribute them by exploiting the recent success of Ocelot's first feature film. *Princes et Princesses* was produced by Les Armateurs, co-produced with La Fabrique, Gebeka, and Studio O. The French director took the opportunity to honour his otherwise unnoticed early works and introduce the public to the lyrical intensity he was capable of. In France alone, it reached eight hundred thousand admissions in cinemas. Years later, the film was still being screened widely, achieving impressive audience results.

THE COLLABORATION WITH BJÖRK

In 2007, the director was contacted by the popular Icelandic singer Björk. She and her young daughter loved Kirikou, and Björk wanted Ocelot to direct the music video for one of the singles from her new album *Volta*. At the time, the filmmaker was auditioning dancers for the musical *Kirikou et Karabà*, so he had just met Legrand Bemba-Debert, the dancer who would play Kirikou in the theatre production. As Björk had a particular interest in Kirikou, Ocelot proposed Legrand Bemba-Debert as the lead in the video. Once the very few coordinates of the project had been agreed upon, the work was left completely in Ocelot's hands, Björk decided to give him complete freedom, despite this being his first experience with music videos. The schedule was tight, the filmmaker told the production company that he could start filming in June. He was asked to deliver in May. As an artist of Björk's calibre, he agreed to deliver a month before filming was due to start.

The *Earth Intruders* video could be completed in such a short period of time because of the use of a combination of live-action, silhouette animation, 3D computer graphics, traditional animation, cutouts, and other special effects. The video shows the singer's face floating in the background with her eyes closed, while in the foreground a group of warriors in silhouette dance to the music and fight each other. Björk's face is blurred by an iridescent marbled pattern that slowly changes colour as the figures move. The video ends with Björk's face in the middle of a cold-toned landscape, slowly opening her eyes as she sings the last verse of the lyrics. The figures in the foreground were obtained by replicating the silhouette of Legrand Bemba-Debert, previously filmed and wearing a costume based on a model by Anne-Lise Koehler, which was, in turn, based on Ocelot's design (Figure 2.8).

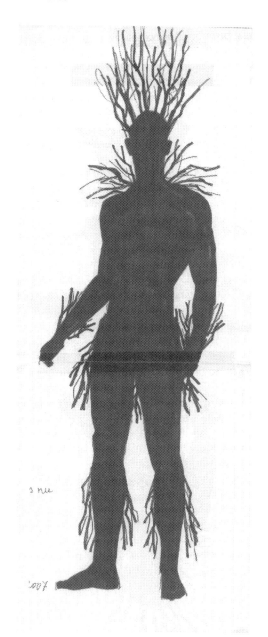

FIGURE 2.8 Costume study for Björk music video *Earth Intruders*. Felt pen on paper, 2007. © Ocelot-Studio O.

Despite the use of live-action and the addition of small do-it-yourself tricks and special effects, the video respects the fundamentals of the silhouette film. The space is organised in two non-communicating two-dimensional planes and a left-to-right movement is also maintained, being that the video has a long sideways tracking shot to accompany the progress of the action. The director mainly used black silhouettes because he was familiar with all the shortcuts they could offer. The video was delivered on time and Björk expressed great enthusiasm. The collaboration was a success, and the two great artists mutually benefitted from one another's freedom and profound creativity.

NOTES

1. Jouvanceau, Pierre. *Il cinema di silhouette*. Recco: Le mani, 2004, p. 118.
2. Ben Nun, Yaël et al, *op. cit.*, p. 56.
3. Ibid.
4. Personal communication with Bénédicte Galup, 9 March 2023.
5. Ibid.
6. Ben Nun, Yaël et al, op. cit., p. 19.
7. Interview by Giannalberto Bendazzi on the occasion of the 11th edition of AniFest, Teplice, Czech Republic, 26 April–1 May 2012.
8. Neupert, Richard. *French Animation History*. Oxford; Malden: Wiley-Blackwell, 2011, p. 132.
9. Bazou, Sébastien. "Princes et Princesses: Les contes de fées revisités". January 5, 2011, in *ArteFake*.
10. Barthes, Roland. *Image, Music, Text*. London: Fontana Press, 1977, p. 146.
11. Neupert, Richard, *op. cit.*, p. 132.
12. Ibid.
13. Duggan, Anne. "The Fairy-Tale Film in France: Postwar Reimaginings". in Zipes, Jack; Greenhill, Pauline; Magnus-Johnston, Kendra. *Fairy-Tale Films Beyond Disney: International Perspectives*. New York; London: Routledge, 2015, p. 78.
14. "Michel Ocelot aux Cinemas Studio in Tours, France. Film Presentation: *Ivan Tsarevitch et la Princesse Changeante* aux cinémas Studio de Tours". October 2, 2016.

15. "Michel Ocelot, l'inventeur", conversation between Michel Ocelot and Hervé Joubert-Laurencin at the 4th professional meeting on animated film writing in Fontevraud, October 9, 2015.
16. Ibid.
17. Neupert, Richard, *op. cit.* p. 133.
18. "An Extensive Personal Interview with Director Michel Ocelot". August 29, 2008, in *GhibliWorld*.
19. Zipes, Jack. *The Enchanted Screen: The Unknown History of Fairy Tale Films*. New York; London: Routledge, 2010, p. 19.
20. Ben Nun, Yaël et al, *op. cit.*, p. 28.
21. King, C. Richard; Bloodsworth-Lugo, Mary K.; Lugo-Lugo, Carmen R. *Animating Difference: Race, Gender, and Sexuality in Contemporary Films for Children*. Lanham, Md.: Rowman & Littlefield, 2010, p. 50.
22. Jouvanceau, Pierre, *op. cit.*, p. 84.
23. Ben Nun, Yaël et al, *op. cit.*, p. 47.
24. Master-Class by Michel Ocelot moderated by Vanessa Tonnini on the occasion of Movie Up 2020, 27 October 2018.
25. Ben Nun, Yaël et al, *op. cit.*, p. 48.
26. Jouvanceau, Pierre, *op. cit.*, p. 193.
27. Van Brabant, Louise. *La part de l'ombre: Michel Ocelot ou la réappropriation de l'espace dans le film de silhouettes*. Master Thesis, Université de Liège, Liège, 2017, p. 40.
28. Jouvanceau, Pierre, *op. cit.*, p. 133.
29. "Le zootrope épatant", in *Fluide Glacial*, n. 66. Paris: Audie, December 1981, p. 42–43.
30. Jouvanceau, Pierre, *op. cit.*, pp. 137–140.
31. Van Brabant, Louise, *op. cit.*, p. 47.
32. Neupert, Richard. "Kirikou and the animated figure/body", in *Studies in French Cinema*, 8(1), Taylor & Francis, 2008, p. 47.
33. "Les Contes de la Nuit. Dossier de presse." Nord-Ouest Films.
34. Ibid.
35. Ibid.
36. Sifianos, George. "Une technique idéale", in *Positif*, Paris: Scope, 1991, p. 102.
37. "Dragons et Princesses. Dossier de presse."
38. Ben Nun, Yaël et al, *op. cit.*, p. 52.
39. "Critique D'autres films", in *Libération*, 20 July 2011.
40. Rigouste, Paul. "Les Contes de la nuit (2011): Le sexisme archaïque de Michel Ocelot", in *Le cinéma est politique*, 26 July 2012.
41. "Les Contes de la Nuit. Dossier de presse." Nord-Ouest Films.

CHAPTER 3

Once Upon a Time, Kirikou

THE BIRTH OF KIRIKOU

In the mid-1990s Michel Ocelot had gained a certain notoriety and esteem in the niche world of animation, such that in 1994 he was elected president of the Association Internationale du Film d'Animation (the International Animated Film Association – ASIFA). ASIFA was founded in 1960 in Annecy, France. Founding members included John Halas and Norman McLaren, who was elected as the association's first president. In cooperation with UNESCO, ASIFA endeavoured to unite the animation world in peace and find ways for animators from both sides of the Iron Curtain to meet in person. The main goal of the association was to promote the sharing of animated films and develop enduring international friendships.[1] The French director presided over this prestigious position until 1999, when he decided to resign to dedicate all his time to his projects. In the mid-1990s, he had also begun working on his first feature film, an exciting adventure that would lead to the creation of his most famous character: Little Kirikou. The small hero's fame is boundless, and his birth marked a turning point in the animator's career. Nevertheless, this would probably not have been possible without the fundamental

DOI: 10.1201/9781003292173-4

contribution of the producer Didier Brunner, who steered the animator towards creating his first feature film. After working for a few years in the film industry as an assistant director and then as a documentarist, Brunner founded the production company Trans-Europe Film in 1987, specifically targeting animation. Trans-Europe produced Ocelot's series *Les Contes de la Nuit*, in 1992.

During his periods of unemployment, Ocelot continued to write and draw incessantly. When Brunner asked him for a story, the author managed to write a complete one in just one week, drawing on the many cues and drafts he had gathered over the years. Ocelot had long nurtured a strong desire to tell a story set in Africa, re-calling the feelings of extraordinary awe and fascination during his joyous childhood in Guinea. Brunner had in the meantime left Trans-Europe to found a new own production company at the beginning of 1994 – Les Armateurs, with the aim of developing a genuine auteur approach in animated cinema. The producer had the foresight to realise in the early 1990s that audiences' taste was changing and that the demand for quality animated film products would grow in the following years. The encounter with Ocelot marked the beginning of something that would exceed the ex-pectations of both of them: The making of *Kirikou et la Sorcière* (*Kirikou and the Sorceress* – 1998) (Figure 3.1).

Apart from taking complete charge of the direction of the film, Ocelot was responsible for much of its making. Screenplay, dialogue, storyboard, and graphic design for the eventual one thousand two hundred shots were all created by him. With regard to the script, the author took inspiration from a West African tale, part of a 1912 collection of stories gathered by the writer and ethnologist François-Victor Équilbecq,[2] circulating throughout French territories at the time he lived in Guinea. The animator was thunderstruck by the story's incipit and decided to keep it in its entirety. The tale and the movie thus share the same beginning: A baby talking in his mother's womb and giving birth to himself. From then on, the screenplay was completely written by the director, eliminating some elements and adding others.

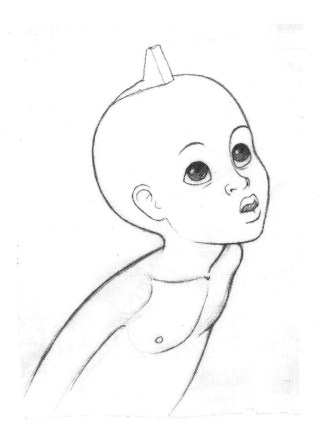

FIGURE 3.1 Kirikou, character study sketch. *Kirikou et la Sorcière*, 1998. © Ocelot-Studio O.

The film takes place, in an undefined distant past, in a traditional African village subjugated by the powers of the fearsome sorceress Karabà and her army of robot-like *fétiches*. The water sources have dried up and all the men in the village have been devoured by the sorceress. Newly born infant Kirikou decides to confront her, but unlike the other villagers the child asks a fundamental question, "Why is Karabà wicked?". Guided by his doubt and with the sole help of his cunning and intelligence, Kirikou is able to save the villagers from the consequences of the sorceress' spells. With the help of the wise grandfather, he also discovers the secret of Karabà's wickedness: A thorn stuck in her back by a group of men. Kirikou manages to remove the thorn. After helping the sorceress to heal, Karabà kisses Kirikou, who suddenly becomes a strong and handsome young man. After a hug, the couple returns to the village, followed by the men, whom Karabà did not devour, but had imprisoned and turned into her fétiches. Finally freed from her spell, they can return to their families in an atmosphere of festive reconciliation.

Ocelot again approached the rich and multifaceted universe of the traditional tale, bringing as he did to his previous shorts an original and fresh point of view. The animator repeatedly related his disappointment at seeing his works consistently aimed exclusively at an audience of children. In fact, it is only in recent years that animation has begun, with difficulty, to break free from the stereotypical notion of its being a product solely for children. The French director, likewise, had to undergo this simplification, in part further corroborated by his extensive use of the fairy tale as the main structure of his stories. To Ocelot, immersion in the world of traditional tales was not a shortcut to accessing a child audience, but rather a means of giving his stories a universal scope and allowing him to communicate with widely different people. His ability as a storyteller made the feature film unforgettable, gaining acclaim from young and old alike. The director succeeded in addressing children without patronising them and enthralling adults by loading the tale with symbolic meanings and subtexts (Figure 3.2).

Over the original tale, the filmmaker decided on some narrative choices that allowed him to deal with various themes he considered fundamental. Nonetheless, the script retains the core of some key concepts frequently repeated in traditional African tales. Intelligence and cunning prevailing over physical strength, the value of younger people, and the importance of listening to elders

FIGURE 3.2 *Kirikou et la Sorcière*, 1998. Kirikou's birth. Gouache on cel and paper. Musée-Château d'Annecy collection.

are all recurring themes in the African oral storytelling tradition.[3] Far from being an adaptation of the original tale, it is instead a reworking so profound as to transform it into a totally different story. With the aim of universalising the scope of the story, he also drew on the European repertoire, such as the fairy tales of Perrault and the Brothers Grimm. The original names were replaced by others invented by the author so that anyone could identify with the characters. The name Kirikou replaced the original Amadou, a name quite common in West African countries. The character of the mother, who disappears in the tale after giving birth, is maintained throughout the film, making the woman a relevant figure in the narrative and allowing the author to deal with the theme of the mother-child relationship. Kirikou's mother is a charming figure, with a calm, forceful personality; she is a clever and insightful advisor and also remarkably tender with her little son. The moment in which the child, having finally made water gush out of the spring and apparently drowned to death, reopens his eyes after being embraced by his mother is one of the most moving scenes in the entire film.

The ending of the original tale was also radically altered. While the protagonist of the original tale kills the sorceress, Kirikou chooses to understand the causes of her evil, help her and unite with her. Kirikou's stubborn curiosity allowed the author to explore complex themes without resorting to simplistic stereotypes and typical patterns. One of the most captivating moments is Kirikou's dialogue with his grandfather, in which the revered sage identifies fear and superstitious beliefs as the root of Karabà's power, inviting us not to stop at the surface. Kirikou's grandfather embodies the figure of the wise old man and the role of the helper, revealing to the infant the secret behind Karabà's wickedness. Karabà is an intensely fascinating antagonist. She undergoes a rapid, yet very significant transformation arc at the end of the film. Her wickedness is provoked by a traumatic experience: A rape by a group of men, symbolised by the thorn stuck in her back. Thus, the event is readable on several levels, making it acceptable for an audience of children, but at the same time meaningful and relatable for adults. Her story makes Karabà a villain outside the rigid schemes of good and evil that recur both in traditional fairy tales and in animated films for the mass audiences up to that time. What is somewhat jarring, conversely, is the dynamic between Kirikou and Karabà in the final passages of the film. Kirikou's sudden growth can definitely be interpreted as a metaphor for his maturation as a result of his support in the physical and psychological healing of the sorceress. Kirikou can become a man worthy of the name insofar as he has redeemed the evil done by other men before him. Nonetheless, the condescension with which the sorceress agrees to partner with the young man traces traditional tropes that see the female figure as a reward at the end of the male hero's journey. This element detracts, in part, from the delicacy with which the story is treated and the remarkable power of its message.

As with some characters in the previous short films, Kirikou has no magical powers and is able to overcome obstacles purely through positive human qualities: Curiosity, courage, and cleverness. The little child is a catalyst hero, as defined by Christopher Vogler.[4] His arc of transformation does not start with the usual goal of resolving himself; rather, he takes on an important mission and sets off on an adventure. In addition to changing himself, his goal is to transform the reality around him. The director's intention was to show the positive consequences of the sincere and persevering attitude displayed by the hero, inviting viewers to confront the world with the same bluntness. As pointed out by Gilles Ciment, "The main attraction of the story does not lie in a moral for its own sake, but rather in the approach of the little hero".[5] And since the filmmaker considers Kirikou to be his alter ego, his direct and forthright approach reflects Ocelot's relationship with animated cinema. The sincerity with which Kirikou addressed the world resembles the honesty and pureness with which Ocelot approaches his creations, a reason why, according to the director, the film has captivated and impressed such a wide audience.[6]

Kirikou was completely invented by Ocelot and is very similar in attitude and relational dynamics to Gédéon, who was equally generous and crafty. Among the sources of inspiration is Leuk-le-Lièvre,[7] the protagonist of a collection of short stories set in Africa, written by Senegalese authors and teachers Léopold Sédar Senghor and Abdoulaye Sadji. The book was published in 1953 and circulated in the following years in schools throughout all the French colonial territories. Young Michel read it during his childhood. In the book, emphasis is placed on moral qualities, such as intelligence and wisdom, which enable the characters to cope with difficult situations.

Curiously enough, one of Kirikou's most fascinating characteristics arose for technical reasons, namely his running very fast. At the beginning of the story, it was necessary for the child to catch up with his uncle who had already set out for Karabà's hut to confront her. In order to allow the main character's meeting with the uncle, it was necessary to find a solution.

FIGURE 3.3 Sketch of Kirikou for the film's poster. *Kirikou et les Hommes et les Femmes*, 2012. © Ocelot-Studio O.

Ocelot, therefore, decided to make him run very quickly, and this element was retained in the entire film, becoming one of the distinguishing features of the little hero (Figure 3.3).

The existence of the fétiches also originated for technical reasons. Karabà is a highly elaborated figure, rich in fine decorations. In particular, the jewellery is strikingly described in detail to emphasise her elegance and regality. However, all of this was very difficult and expensive to animate, so the director decided to have her stand motionless while the small robots did everything for her. The fétiches were later identified as the men who disappeared from the village at the hands of the sorceress, an element that allowed for an additional enrichment to the ending. In fact, in the transition from a script initially conceived as a short to a feature-length film plot, the return of the freed men to the village enabled the narration to be lengthened and made the conclusion of the story more coherent.

The script has a simple and linear progression, the pace is slow, and the narration is reduced to the essentials. The graphic

FIGURE 3.4 *Kirikou et la Sorcière*. Initial concept. Ink, gouache, and paper cut on cel and paper, 1998. © Ocelot-Studio O.

style similarly is quite synthetic. The filmmaker was initially geared to create a story depicted with a 1920s aesthetic, with bodies stylised and outlined as black silhouettes on which the ornaments consisting of jewellery would stand out (Figure 3.4).

The producer asked Ocelot to make compromises and create a film with more classical visual traits; therefore, Ocelot switched to cel animation. This compelled choice proved to be a source of great expressive potential. With colour, the human figures began to take on a more believable form and allowed the director to achieve a strong humanisation of the characters.[8] Although the shift to cel animation meant that Ocelot had to move closer to an approach of realistic representation, the influence of his previous experience with silhouettes is clearly visible in this film. The characters are two-dimensional, delineated through the use of a few flat, uniform colours, and outlined by a very pronounced contour line. They maintain an effect of marked artificiality since there is no emphasis on the representation of volume and there are few elements of reference to the three-dimensionality of space. As already experienced with silhouette animation, the characters are often depicted in profile, the figures tend to move from one side of the screen to the other, and spatial depth is suggested through the mere overlapping of figures and background, or between various characters. As stated Yves Schaëffner in his review:

> The characters, far from tending towards an artificial three-dimensionality, are distinguished from the background through the contrast of colours. In no way does the author aspire to perfectly imitate reality. It is through the atmosphere, the play of colours and the expressions on faces that he gives these characters depth.[9]

Ocelot drew the storyboard and spent several months working on the visual design of the characters and sets. The filmmaker always preferred to refer to the storyboard with the word *scenarimage*, since sketches, sound, and technical cues are combined and he liked to take care of all of them.[10] The storyboard creation work was completed entirely by the filmmaker, although initially the producers, who did not trust him enough, asked that it be redrawn by some experts. Once it was realised that a more-complex storyboard would be extremely difficult to animate, they reverted to the one designed by Ocelot (Figure 3.5).

The study of the characters included a careful analysis of photographs and postcards collected by the author, before moving on to sketches and then to the final design, which gradually improved as the storyboard was created. Helped by Bénédicte Galup, Eric Serre, and Anne-Lise Koehler, the director took care of creating the rotation models of the characters, the animals, and the props – a term used to designate objects in movies, animated or not. Rotation models consist of drawings showing each character from the front, back, profile, and three-quarter view,

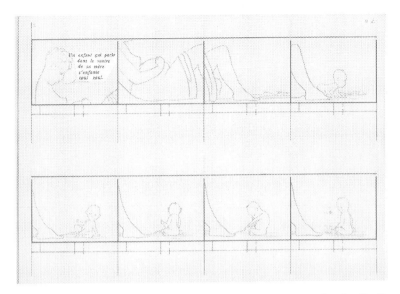

FIGURE 3.5 *Kirikou et la Sorcière*. Storyboard, 1998. © Ocelot-Studio O.

indicating how to draw their main gestures and different expressions. As already mentioned, the Karabà figure remained as originally conceived, but the other characters underwent some modifications due to the constraints of animation (Figure 3.6).

The mother's hairstyle, initially conceived with an elaborate braid on the forehead, was simplified, and the same was done for the grandfather's headgear. Its final appearance, although similar to the headgear of the pharaohs of ancient Egypt, was inspired by a sixteenth-century bronze from Benin.[11] It was crucial for the director to draw his inspiration from African art, so the creative process began with documentation work. The figurative sources are in some cases very precise but always marked by the personal touch of the author, who drew from this vast and varied figurative culture. The result was a syncretic aesthetic, characterised by synthesis and linearism, in some cases blending African art with features typical of the early twentieth-century artistic avant-gardes.

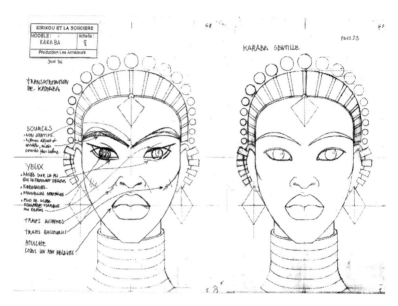

FIGURE 3.6   Study for Karabà's transformation. *Kirikou et la Sorcière,* 1998. © Ocelot-Studio O.

The appearance of the fétiches draws on traditional African sculpture, combining different styles from various parts of Africa. To add a touch of harshness, befitting servants of an evil sorceress, Ocelot emphasised the contrasts and sharpened the edges. The same happened with the external decorative elements of the sorceress' hut, achieving a final effect similar to the visual brutality of the German expressionist avant-garde group Die Brücke. The fétiches, particularly the one tasked with guarding the sorceress' dwelling, also display an interesting mixture of technology and primitivism reminiscent of some early twentieth-century works such as those of the French painter Fernand Léger. The resulting stylistic intersection can be found both in the treatment of the backgrounds of *Kirikou et la Sorcière* and in the scenery of later movies. Also striking in its didactic nature is the symbolic use of colours, especially for the figure of Karabà, always framed by bright reds and surrounded by a desolate,

FIGURE 3.7 *Kirikou et la Sorcière*, 1998. © Les Armateurs / Odec Kid Cartoons / France 3 Cinéma / Monipoly / Trans Europe Film / Exposure / RTBF / Studio O.

lifeless land, played out in shades of grey and black. In the last scenes as soon as the sorceress enters the forest we see the vegetation fading around her. In the scenes following her healing, the scenery is transformed into a plethora of soothing shades of white, green, pale blue and deep blue (Figure 3.7).

The study of the backgrounds represented the opportunity for the filmmaker to give vent to his predilection for vivid decorativism. The set design was entrusted to Anne-Lise Koehler and Thierry Million. Ocelot's instructions for the representation of vegetation were not to spare any effort but to create a small piece of art for each individual plant. He required great attention to detail, combining botanical accuracy with a stylisation typical of Egyptian art and with colours inspired by the works of the French painter Henri Rousseau. Wherever possible, the director tried to draw inspiration from African art. For the backgrounds, the choice fell on Rousseau, as there are only very rare examples of paintings from Africa:

I knew for the architecture, the fabrics, the sculpture, the decoration and the jewellery what was needed. But I had no images. There is no African painting. Thanks to the Douanier Rousseau I found exactly what I needed. [...] I worked à la Douanier Rousseau with delight, he uses quite a lot of gradiation in his plants, that is what makes his paintings iridescent and appealing.[12]

The sets were hand drawn and then coloured by colourists, in some cases by hand with gouache or watercolours, in other cases with the aid of computer tools. Individually drawn elements were then assembled and multiplied to allow the creation of more complex scenery, such as the forests (Figure 3.8).

Bénédicte Galup was in charge of compositing, a phase that included scanning the drawings, colouring them, and eventually creating the final images. These were created by bringing together all the elements that make up a shot: The sets, animation, choice of framing, any camera movements, special effects, and rendering, using TicTacToon software.[13] Ocelot described the assembly of the first sets as one of the most exciting steps:

[A] moment when our creation struck us, when we called on everyone, was the first forest assembled. All the elements of the sets were drawn and watercoloured. My recommendation to the designers was that each plant in the forest should be a masterpiece. [...] The instructions had been followed and I could see a beautiful and delicate herbarium coming together. but I didn't know what all this, digitised, multiplied and crammed on the screen, would look like. And one day Thierry called us. On the monitor there was a forest that left us speechless.[14]

For a low-budget film, its production was particularly complex. After two years spent recovering funds, implementation took four years. Initially, the early stages of processing took place

FIGURE 3.8   Flowers study. *Kirikou et la Sorcière*, 1998. © Ocelot-Studio O.

in Ocelot's Paris apartment, which was converted into a make-shift studio for the purpose. When a semblance of routine allowed the crew to tackle the more artistic part of the adventure, they decided to move to Angoulême, at the time an area completely foreign to animation. As Galup recounted:

> There were no studios yet, but generous new friends to take you in. To move the production, we filled my car with drawing boxes and with Michel we left for the Charente. The rest of the crew joined us shortly thereafter. A small studio had been set up in a residence and we rented a large house where we were all roommates. In time Angoulême would prove to be the right choice.[15]

Then, the work was distributed over six locations in five different countries. It was divided between Angoulême – where Les Armateurs set up a studio, with a crew directed by Bénédicte Galup – and Brussels, in the Odec Kids Cartoons studio. Two studios in Eastern Europe were later contacted to handle the animation phases: Exist Studio, located in Budapest, Hungary, and Rija Studio, based in Riga, Latvia. Almost all of the animation took place in Riga, initially creating some difficulties, given the inexperience of the animation crew who were used to smaller projects. The director remembers with particular fondness his relationship with the Latvian team – composed exclusively of women. Ocelot was constantly travelling among the various locations to guide the studio crews, supervise the outcome of the animations, and ensure the coherence of the whole project.

Kirikou et la Sorcière consists of more than two hundred and fifty thousand drawings made exclusively by hand. The process of creating an animated drawing started with an initial sketch, often in blue pencil, followed by a very precise final drawing made to facilitate animation and colouring (Figure 3.9).

The drawings were then scanned and the animation-tested on the computer in a low-definition rendering. However, the

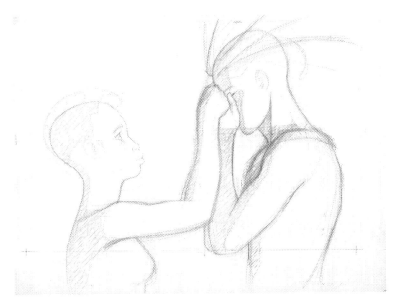

FIGURE 3.9 Young man Kirikou meets his mother. Preparatory drawing. *Kirikou et la Sorcière*, 1998. © Ocelot-Studio O.

movie does not contain any CGI elements, only flat drawings arranged in different layers. Once the animation was completed in studios set in Riga and Budapest, the material was supervised by the director and the supervision crew in France, then distributed between France and Belgium to complete the filming, which was done with the help of computer-based tools. Each picture is composed of many elements – several layers of sets, props, and characters in varying numbers. Computer filming enabled the assembling of all the final elements of the film. This was carried out mainly in the studio of Odec Kid Cartoons in Bruxelles, where post-production, editing, and sound design also took place. The final result is a cinematic product visually rich and sparkling, although the animation is often evidently limited.

For the recording of the original voices and soundtrack, Ocelot decided to travel to Dakar, Senegal, as the author wanted a dubbing with good French, but with a West African accent. The director had to overcome the misgivings of some of the producers, who objected to the recording of dialogue in Africa, as they argued that the public would not like the marked accents. They would have preferred to have Kirikou dubbed by an adult woman, as is often the case with child voices, and hire French voice actors. The filmmaker had to struggle, but eventually, he achieved everything he desired. The young hero was dubbed in Dakar by a nine-year-old boy, who did not have a very strong accent, but priority was given to the best dubbing performance. Karabà was voiced by Senegalese actress Awa Sène Sarr; Kirikou's mother by Franco-Burkinabe actress Maimouna N'Diaye; the grandfather by the actor Robert Liensol, who was in his seventies. Similarly, English dubbing was recorded in South Africa to achieve an analogous result.

The same happened with the soundtrack. The producers tried to convince Ocelot to have it composed and recorded in Paris. The author did not compromise and contacted the Senegalese musician Youssou N'Dour. The singer at the time was already well known internationally and his notoriety helped popularise Senegalese folk music around the world. In his home country, Senegal, and in the rest of Africa he was enjoying exceptional fame, a popularity that was also expanding to Western countries following his 1994 hit with Neneh Cherry, *7 Seconds*. Youssou N'Dour had received many film scripts, but *Kirikou et la Sorcière* was the only one that attracted his attention, and he gladly agreed to contribute. He said that the reasons were twofold:

> Firstly because it is an African story that I felt was very close to me and my sensibility. It tells [...] things that are part of our mythology, our roots. Secondly, because it allowed me to work again in a context of traditional music. It was a precise wish of the director: To avoid modern instruments, percussions, and to find a more

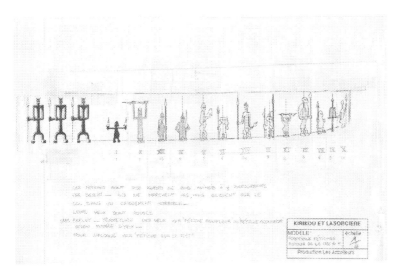

FIGURE 3.10   Les Fètiches. *Kirikou et la Sorcière*, 1998. © Ocelot-Studio O / Musée-Chateau d'Annecy.

natural inspiration, linked to the roots of the music. So we used traditional African instruments such as the bafalon, ritti, cora, xalam, tokho, sabaar and belon.[16]

Moreover, the restriction on the use of percussion instruments traditionally played by men, also took on narrative relevance, since these would not appear until the very last scenes, along with the men abducted by the sorceress returning to the village. As a result, the sound is one of the most fascinating and convincing aspects of the entire film. As Elvis Mitchell remarked, "It's wonderful and rare to see an African landscape rendered for an animated film and not have any of the characters voiced by white mainstream American movie stars, or hear any Broadway approximations of African music"[17] (Figure 3.10).

AN ALTERNATIVE TO DISNEY

When Ocelot and Brunner met in 1990, the international animation film industry was largely dominated by US productions.

Although after Walt Disney's death in 1966, the world animation giant entered a period of crisis that would last around twenty years, in both the US and Europe the Disney cartoon continued to be the hegemonic aesthetic and commercial reference point. The standards of animation in the Western world had also been shaping increasingly downward, conforming its quality to the most commercially advantageous products: Television series, produced mainly in the US and Japan. In this regard, the widespread infiltration of Japanese anime into the commercial television series sector in both France and the rest of Europe had contributed to acclimatising viewers to repetitive and low-quality products.

By the early 1990s, however, the international animation scene was transforming. The decade was a turning point for animation on a global level. The disintegration of state funding systems in the former Soviet Union and satellite countries caused the number of film products in those areas to drop dramatically. Meanwhile, in the US, after years of decline, Disney studios had regained interest in feature film production. The process culminated in the release of *The Little Mermaid* in 1989 (John Musker, Ron Clements) – considered to be the film that marked the renewal of the great animation giant – and it was consecrated with the 1991 blockbuster *Beauty and the Beast* (Gary Trousdale, Kirk Wise), which would set the pace for the company's later years. In the US, the offerings began to diversify with the advent of other big studios, such as DreamWorks and 20th Century Fox's animated film division, albeit mostly flattened on a stereotypical visual and narrative style. Further complicating the picture was the advent of the first animation movies made with computer graphics, which, particularly after the great success of *Toy Story* (John Lasseter) in 1995, would become an additional competitor within the traditional animation industry. On the other hand, in the mid-1990s the first films of the Japanese Studio Ghibli began to circulate in Europe, setting an alternative path marked by quality without compromise.[18]

France had a long history of creating fascinating and innovative animated films, however, the national industry was

historically based on a system of small studios, or even productions by individual filmmakers.[19] Ocelot's first steps into the
world of animation also shared the independent spirit of other
authors such as Paul Grimault, René Laloux, and Jean-François
Laguionie, who had produced a number of short and feature
films with great difficulty between the 1960s and 1980s. The
struggles that many individual animators before Ocelot had
encountered in the preceding years had now conferred upon
French directors what Neupert described as a mixture of
"excitement and frustration within French animation"[20] and
which was also quite evident in the attitude of the novice filmmaker. Nonetheless, with Brunner's crucial input, Ocelot proved
that an alternative to Disney was possible and that it was con-
ceivable to make a wide audience love a sophisticated film
characterised by its authorial visual style and unconventionality
of the plot, furthermore making a financial profit.

Critics uniformly agree the production of *Kirikou et la
Sorcière* was crucial for the impressive renaissance of the French
animation industry. In the early 1990s, the animated feature film
practically did not exist in France – the last relevant product may
have been Paul Grimault's *Le Roi et L'Oiseau* (*The King and the
Mockingbird*) released in 1979. Whereas at that moment producing a feature film appeared an impossible feat, with only one
movie produced in 1990, eight films and seven films were produced in 2003 and 2006, respectively. In 2007, France became the
third-largest animation-producing country in the world, after
the US and Japan.[21] It is also not disputed that Ocelot's first
feature film provided a model for the production of other French
movies in the following years, so much so as to pose the statement "before and after Kirikou". The consequences of this first
step towards the production of auteur films for a wide audience
were extremely positive, ushering in a season of great masterpieces of French animation including *Les Triplettes de
Belleville* (*The Triplets of Belleville* – Sylvain Chomet, 2003);
Persepolis (Marjane Satrapi, 2007); and *Ernest et Célestine* (*Ernest

& *Célestine* – Stéphane Aubier, Vincent Patar and Benjamin Renner, 2012). The company Les Armateurs was, furthermore, a co-producer of some gems of contemporary European animated cinema, such as *The Secret of Kells* (Tomm Moore, Nora Twomey, 2009) and *Les hirondelles de Kaboul* (*The Swallows of Kabul* – Zabou Breitman, Eléa Gobé Mévellec, 2019), made through international partnerships.

Kirikou et la Sorcière was a low-budget film. To produce the feature, it was necessary to convince many stakeholders. Finding the budget was extremely complex, as the film was seen by investors as an auteur project and therefore poorly marketable. The first funds raised were an advance on receipts from the Centre National de la Cinématographie (CNC) of 2.2 million francs, thanks to a financial device created in the 1960s by the CNC. These were supplemented by a contribution of 3.5 million francs from the Canal+ channel.[22] The rest of the budget was raised internationally, distributing the production between France, Belgium, and Luxembourg. The film also benefitted from the support of several public institutions and from the "cartoon plan", an initiative that European Commission's Media Program had put in place since the late 1980s to revitalise the animated film industry in Europe. The final budget was 3.8 million euros,[23] a paltry sum when compared, for instance, with the 90 million dollars spent to finance Disney's *Mulan* (1998, Barry Cook, Tony Bancroft), which was released in theatres at the same time as *Kirikou et la Sorcière*. The distribution of the film was entrusted to a small distributor founded in 1997 in Lyon – Gebeka Films – and supported by the Association française des cinémas d'art et d'essai. The distributor intended to propose quality movies for a young audience and played a central role in the film's success.

There were no financial resources to pay for advertisement, thus it was decided to rely on word of mouth to circulate the film, which surprisingly worked wonderfully. As Ocelot recalls, the distributor Marc Bonny "personally telephoned the cinema exhibitors and convinced them to screen the sixty copies we had managed to make (without any advertisements, trailers or posters). With the first takings, instead of printing advertisements, Bonny decided to print other copies".[24]

"We started with sixty copies versus the six hundred copies of the American films ... we finished at one hundred and sixty copies, but Kirikou never stopped going around, whereas the American films lasted a couple of months and then disappeared".[25] Ocelot insisted that the film be released on the same day as Mulan and within days of Dreamworks' *The Prince of Egypt* (Brenda Chapman, Steve Hickner, Simon Wells – 1998). *Kirikou et la Sorcière* had to fight its way along between two giants, and it prevailed because of the freshness of its protagonist, the striking power of its messages, and the magnificence of its scenery. The movie was seen by one million eight hundred thousand viewers. It was an astounding success, since producer Brunner had expected to sell three hundred thousand tickets in France.[26] The film was honoured with numerous awards at festivals, including the prestigious Grand Prix at Annecy. Between 1998 and 2004 it was distributed in about forty countries and translated into more than twenty-five languages.

As is often the case with artistic products destined to be remembered, the film's success depended not only on its outstanding quality but also on a combination of numerous other factors. The historic moment was particularly favourable on an international level, given the new economic order being reshaped globally. The rise of French animated films in Europe was unmatched, yet a similar revival of the industry can also be detected in other countries. In Italy, for instance, economic awakening followed the foundation of Lanterna Magica production company and the release of *La Freccia Azzurra* (*How the Toys Saved Christmas* – 1996) and *La Gabbianella e il Gatto* (*Lucky and Zorba* – 1998) both directed by Enzo d'Alò. The new offer consisted of auteur animated feature films, aimed at large audiences, which enjoyed wide public and critical acclaim. The impact on the animation industry, albeit on a much smaller scale, was similar to that of the French phenomenon.[27] In addition, the choice of subject, which doubtlessly depended on the author's biography, was particularly felicitous at a time when cultural diversity in the animated image was of greater interest.

In his book *Undoing Culture. Globalization, Postmodernism, and Identity*, Mike Featherstone noted how it was no longer possible to conceive global processes in the dialectic of the dominance of a single centre over the peripheries. Rather, there were different centres that were effecting transformations in the geopolitical balance, and our image of culture depended on it. Culture had become more complex and multifaceted. Without necessarily shifting the favoured centre of cultural production away from the West, the dominant countries had to consider the new actors emerging in the culturally globalised world.[28] This fundamental trait of postmodern culture had also impacted commercial animated films. Not surprisingly, in the years before *Kirikou et la Sorcière* was released, Disney produced several movies considering the globalisation of culture and markets. *Aladdin*, *The Lion King*, and *Mulan* were all products of this new cultural climate. Ocelot's cinematic gem fits perfectly into that trend, capturing the spirit of the moment and also benefiting from greater freedom than Disney's colossals. As the French filmmaker repeated in many interviews:

> I have the great power to be small and free, Disney is big, a slave to the board and to success; in short, it doesn't have the freedom to do what I do even though it has more means. That's the curse of big industry and it's a shame because Disney was a great producer and I have great memories of the old films.[29]

THE SUCCESS OF KIRIKOU

Over the years, among the remarks repeatedly made to Ocelot during interviews about *Kirikou et la Sorcière*, one was particularly recurrent: "You must have been surprised by Kirikou's success". The director always replied that he was prepared both for sensational success and striking failure. However, he also reported how surprised he was by the depth of the movie's success. The critical reception was hugely positive. The feature film toured at the most important animation festivals around the world and was favourably reviewed in both the general and specialised press. Journalists applauded the film's originality, often in comparison with US cartoons. As Jacques Mandelbaum wrote in Le Monde, the film differed "from the traditional celluloid behemoths that arrive at this time of year, simply because by showing things differently, it says something else, thinks another way, dreams another way".[30] In addition to France, the film was also a blockbuster in some other European countries, particularly Italy and Germany, becoming a childhood classic across the continent. In Norway, it was used to teach French to schoolchildren. As the director recalled, "Norwegian children speak French with Senegalese accent!"[31] In Japan, it was adapted into Japanese by Isao Takahata and distributed by the renowned Studio Ghibli.

Unfortunately, distributing the film abroad was not always easy. In Africa, the film's release was affected by the distribution difficulties on the continent. "The film was not seen enough, even though it could have met with an enthusiastic audience",[32] recounted Awa Sène Sarr, voice actress for the sorceress. Movie theatres were few and, in many cases, not affordable for a wide audience. The film was shown as part of some festivals, such as in the case of Quintessence, organised by the director Jean Odoutan in Ouidah, Benin. In addition, the French-based association Cinéma numérique ambulant (CNA) travelled to three countries – Mali, Niger, and Benin – to show it on DVD to the local population. Word of mouth also worked particularly well in Africa, thanks, for example, to itinerant singers in Mali who performed the film's songs moving from village to village; a way of spreading the word about the film that harkened back to the roots of orality.[33]

In Anglo-Saxon countries, however, the circulation of the film was strongly inhibited due to cultural barriers. Distribution was hindered in the United Kingdom and the US. The difficulty of distribution in the United States was the result of numerous factors, in some cases at odds with each other. Ocelot reported many times that most of the difficulties were due to the characters' nudity. In fact, the magazine *Variety* wrote, "This is one pic the religious right won't be lining up to see".[34] Distributors in the UK and US went so far as to demand that the nudity of the characters be covered with bras and underwear. Obviously, Ocelot did not agree. Through the depiction of non-sexualised nudity, Ocelot's intention was to contribute to dignifying the representation of Black women, children, and men. He wanted to show "an Africa that wasn't ashamed to have a body".[35] The filmmaker portrayed women of the most disparate ages and bodies, also with the purpose of not censoring the characteristics of the culture represented. At the same time, as Richard Neupert reported, "not everyone on the left would approve of the film either, especially since it is made by a white European male depicting naked Africans who are often superstitious and narrow-minded".[36] In any case, this unforeseen difficulty considerably reduced the film's release in Anglo-Saxon countries and delayed it for several years. It arrived in the US in 2000, and in the UK in 2003. In both countries it was well-received by audiences and critics, yielding festival awards and positive reviews. BBC critic Jamie Russell called it, "one of the most enchanting animated features in quite some time".[37] The film generated great resonance; the director received touching letters over the years from those who had seen themselves mirrored in Kirikou, particularly Afro-descendant people.[38] One of the most emotional outcomes for the director was the news that a psychologist, Véronique Cormon, had begun treating women survivors of gender-based violence through his film. In 2004, Cormon published a book with a foreword by the filmmaker.[39]

Kirikou's fame did not stop in the first few months but continued to generate a following year after year. Besides the two sequel feature films, the character became the protagonist of several children's adventure books by Ocelot with the help of a number of collaborators. In 2007 a theatrical version of the film was created in Lyon and debuted in Paris. The play was conceived and staged by the British choreographer Wayne McGregor with the collaboration of Ocelot. Music was composed by Youssou N'Dour, Rokia Traorè, and Christophe Minck. The dilemma of how to cast such a young protagonist for a musical was solved by turning the child into a puppet. The choreographer and film director thought of bunkaru, the ancient Japanese theatre in which puppets are manipulated on sight. Kirikou's seventy-five-centimetre-tall puppet was animated admirably on stage by a trio of dancers who articulated all his movements. The puppet was animated by hip-hop and contemporary dancers, twins Taiwo and Kehinde Awaiye, and Legrand Bemba-Debert, who lends his voice to Kirikou, under the guidance of puppeteer Simon Rann. Legrand Bemba-Debert also played adult Kirikou, while the sorceress was interpreted by the actress Fatoumata Diawara. The musical was seen by two hundred and forty thousand people in 2007 alone and it returned to theatres of major French cities in subsequent years.[40] In 2011, Michel Ocelot and Legrand Bemba-Debert collaborated again to create a stage adaptation of *Princes et Princesses*. It was a shadow theatre show played by live actors and actresses and has been performed more than six hundred times, captivating almost eight hundred thousand spectators worldwide.

DIFFERENT PERSPECTIVES ON *KIRIKOU ET LA SORCIÉRE*

Twenty years after the film's release in cinemas, *Kirikou et la Sorciére* was still positively talked about. In a 2018 interview, musician and slam poet Abd al Malik described the film as the French director's encouragement to Africans to tell their own stories: "It is a relay that I am handing over to you. Now, to you, tell your stories, because your stories are beautiful".[41] Indeed, the film helped open a debate on the state of animated cinema in Africa, partly contributing to its visibility abroad, as reported in a 2008 article in the magazine *Africultures*. In the article, it is pointed out that *Kirikou et la Sorciére*, even though wasn't produced in Africa, demonstrated that European audiences could be interested in animated movies set in Africa.[42] The feature was also received not only as a positive sign but also as a truthful depiction of rural African reality: "I myself was born under a banana tree, my umbilical cord was cut from a cane!" said Cameroonian Robert Fopa, president de l'Association internationale Culture sans frontière (AICSF). "The midwife who attended the birth then helps educate the child. She tests him. ... Kiriku also evokes today's reality".[43] For Benin film-maker Jean Odoutan, the sorceress Karabà and her small army of fétiches reflected the voodoo and animist environment of a part of his country. He added that this story of heroism and resistance took on special meaning in Ouidah, as it was one of the most active slave trading ports on the continent. Moreover, the film-maker Laurent Chevallier highlighted the importance of the movie for Guinea: "It was the first country to break away from de Gaulle in 1958, and this is still very much alive in people's memories, and Guineans have found an echo of this national pride in Kirikou".[44]

On the other hand, the animator Pierre Sauvalle, co-founder with Aïda Ndiaye of the Senegalese animation studio Pictoon in 1998, took Kirikou as an example to describe the paradox of African culture told by foreigners. In fact, he attributed the distributors' refusal to broadcast in France the animated series *Kabongo le Griot* (Pierre Awoulbe Sauvalle, 2002) to the presence of a modern protagonist, far from the "village imagery" and therefore disturbing.[45] *Kirikou et la Sorciére* is identified thus as the reassuring counterpoint of a highly urbanised and developed vision of Africa, inconceivable to Westerners. His colleague,

Aïda Ndiaye, was of the same opinion. She stated that the movie persisted in a Western vision of the African village. A pleasant sight, but unreal and characterised by refusal of modernity.[46] The same issue is addressed in a highly critical essay on the film, written by Joannesburg-based animator Seni Mtshali.[47] According to Mtshali, the film repurposes a stereotyped and colonial vision of sub-Saharan Africa, conveyed by specific graphic and narrative choices. The movie, by blending themes and repertoires from different countries, would contribute to perpetuating the vision of a continent devoid of significant diverse cultural manifestations and stuck in an indefinite time, where past and present mingle. In particular, the village huts in the film combine different traditional architectural types and the appearance of the uncle warrior garments is a fusion of elements from diametrically opposed cultures. Mtshali's opinion is particularly valuable, as it highlights some rarely analysed features of the film. Indeed, it can be agreed with her how much this flattening is a sign of Ocelot's cultural limitations. It is worth noting how avoiding diversification contributes to a homogeneous and static view of Africa, where cultural and geographic differences are erased. Moreover, Mtshali pointed out that the characterisation of the villagers reproduces stereotypes often attributed to Africans. With the exception of Kirikou and his mother, the characters are portrayed on the one hand as naive, mistrustful, and superstitious; on the other as good dancers and happily festive. In fact, it is arguable how adherence to stereotypes can clearly be detected. However, the portrayal of distrust as a hallmark of all villagers takes on a different meaning when reread in the dynamic of opposition between the main character and the others. This characterisation serves as a metaphor for the representation of a progressive force confronting more reactionary drives. It has a further significance aimed at emphasising the relationship between the wise child and the adult, conservative, population; a literary topos typical of African and European tales. Mtshali concludes that the film is aimed at a purely European audience and therefore not as enjoyable for a viewer from an African country.

In this regard, it is useful to return to the interview with which this section opens, since Abd al Malik also commented on the importance of white children watching the movie and identifying with Kirikou: "Once they would meet the other who does not resemble them outwardly, they will not see the other, but a variant of themselves".[48] *Kirikou et la Sorciére* was, as a matter of fact, modelled for an audience of people born in the West, but not exclusively white. As revealed by the director during some interviews, the film was aimed likewise at Britain and the US, as countries with a large portion of their populations composed of Afro-descendant people. With these premises, and placing the film in the historical and economic context in which it was produced, *Kirikou et la Sorciére* was a groundbreaking movie. Never before had an animated feature film been created with Black protagonists and set in Africa. Like many of Ocelot's stories, it is a film full of positive, edifying messages, and the fact that these came from a Black infant and his community was a complete novelty.

Moreover, the decision to tell a story set in Africa was an opportunity for Ocelot to pay homage to a culture he had known during his childhood and continued to love and respect. As the filmmaker stated, he "needed to settle the sentimental accounts with Africa".[49] He wanted to show the "Africa of the stories because that is what is the beginning of the story, a story, but also the Africa of my childhood".[50] It wasn't the result of mere appropriation nor of a marketing strategy. On the contrary, the director had to struggle from the beginning with the scepticism of the producers who were opposed to an animated film set in Africa, who worried that the characters were too dark-skinned – and in response, he darkened them even more. He had to defend his ideas to the end, including the recording of the soundtrack in Senegal, a choice that set the film in stark contrast to the norm of large productions seen up to then. The narrative material was also treated with extreme delicacy. Ocelot reworked the original tale into a universal story, aimed at a transnational and mixed audience. Thus, the fable is directed at the globalised society described by anthropologist Renato Rosaldo: "All of us inhabit an interdependent late twentieth-century world, which is at once marked by borrowing and lending across porous cultural boundaries, and saturated with inequality, power, and domination".[51]

The complexity of the seemingly simple and straightforward feauture, has led to its becoming an object of study from a postcolonial perspective. As pointed out by Abdou Ngom, Professor at Cheikh Anta Diop University in Dakar, Senegal, the movie could be read through Karabà's politics of subjugation as an allegorical depiction of Western domination adopted during the colonial period.[52] Thus, Karabà's reign of fear could be equated with the strategies of control perpetrated by the West. Demarcating a territory, setting fire to houses, and extorting gold from women were all part of the tactics used to overpower oppressed populations and instil fear in people's minds. Moreover, it is noted how the villagers' ability to counter the sorceress's stratagems by any means emblematises African resistance to centuries of colonial rule. Seen through the lens of postcolonial critique, the return of the elderly repository of wisdom to the village would emphasise the immense potential in the recovery of traditional knowledge by postcolonial societies. Furthermore, the rejection of the manicheist concept of good and evil and the unification of the two antagonistic forces at the end of the film "underscores, in some way, the hybridisation process at the heart of postcolonial theory while repudiating the destructive ethnic, linguistic, geographical, and religious boundaries strategically imposed on African populations by the European colonizer".[53]

AFTER THE NOTORIETY, THE SEQUELS

Following the success of *Kirikou et la Sorciére*, many insisted that Ocelot should direct a sequel. For several years, the filmmaker kept firmly stating that he would not make a second film. The story of

Kirikou was complete as it was; everything had already been told. Eventually, in 2003 he was persuaded to continue and began the production of *Kirikou et les Bêtes Sauvages* (*Kirikou and the Wild Animals* – Michel Ocelot, Bénédicte Galup – 2005). He declared:

> "It wasn't me who decided, but the audience. […] Often, at the end of the shows, there are families who want to see me and ask me to continue. […] Outside the cinemas people come up to me and tell me that I have no right to stop. The child Kirikou did not ask my opinion and I was no match".[54]

Initially, the sequel was supposed to be a series for television, but in the course of development, it was decided to turn it into a feature film for the cinema. The movie was made with practically the same production partnerships as the first, and distributed by Gebeka. As *Azur & Asmar* was already in the works at that time, Ocelot decided to leave a large role to one of his most important collaborators, Bénédicte Galup, who co-directed the movie with him and wrote the synopsis of the tale involving the giraffe (Figure 3.11).

FIGURE 3.11 *Kirikou et les Bêtes Sauvages*, 2005. © Les Armateurs / Gebeka Films / France 3 Cinéma / Studio O.

Kirikou et les Bêtes Sauvages was produced between 2003 and 2005 in three different locations, Angoulême, Latvia, and Vietnam. Once the storyboard was established, the production was divided geographically. Ocelot handled some aspects of the film in Paris, where Azur & Asmar production was located, while Galup worked with her crew in Angoulême and Vietnam. However, the two met regularly to share some phases of the project. The co-direction experience was not among the easiest, and as Galup reported, it sometimes strained their friendship.[55] The production was the result of more than two hundred people employed in fifty professional specialities, distributed in ten production units in three countries. As was the case with the first film, the animations were mainly made in Latvia, with some sequences completed in Vietnam. The preliminary stages and post-production were entrusted to the French team. For the composition of the soundtrack, the director turned to the great Cameroonian saxophonist and composer Manu Dibango. Ocelot had already contacted him for the first film, but Youssou N'Dour's enormous notoriety led the producers to engage him. Therefore, the choice fell on Dibango for this second production set in Africa, while Youssou N'Dour was still present with the previous song and new melodies. There is significantly more music in this movie than in the first one and in this case, the musicians worked closely with Ocelot. It took about eight months to complete the soundtrack and Dibango described the director as "pretty finicky". In an interview, he told of the filmmaker's punctiliousness in the recording of the soundtrack. His search for authenticity led them to record some sounds directly in Africa, as in the case of the birds. Said Dibango, "when Michel wanted birdsong, it had to be recordings of real African birds, not any old birds from anywhere!"[56]

The release date was again set for December, with a total of three hundred copies distributed and a well-developed advertisement apparatus.[57] The film was a success, even greater than the first movie. It was seen by more than two million viewers and also won a few awards. It was distributed abroad in more than fifty countries. A special screening was even organised in Cannes by UNESCO, exclusively for children, where Kirikou welcomed them in twelve languages. As in the case of his predecessor, a large part of the audience were families with children. By the end of the first film, the protagonist was all grown up and on the verge of marriage to Karabà, though the audience was not interested in seeing an adult Kirikou. On the screen, people wanted to see again the child they had loved and eagerly followed. Therefore, *Kirikou et les Bêtes Sauvages* collects four adventures that happened to Kirikou before he freed Karabà from the thorn and the pain that plagued her. The tales are introduced by Kirikou's grandfather, who becomes the narrator of this movie. In the first story, the child defeats a hyena that had destroyed the village vegetable garden. In the second, Kirikou and the villagers try their hand at creating clay artefacts that they then sell at the market. In the third story, the infant discovers new landscapes and significant locations in Africa on the back of a giraffe. In the fourth tale, Kirikou succeeds with the help of the other children in healing their respective mothers who were victims of a poisonous flower. Karabà had hidden it in a barrel of freshly brewed beer that the women had tasted, intending to poison them. The author kept the same characters from the first film, focusing more on the relationships between the villagers and adding little curiosities about village life. Kirikou's short adventures are engaging and retain the freshness of the character's first appearance on screen. In particular, the episode involving Kirikou and the giraffe adds an extra touch of awe by showing new scenarios and natural wonders. The animation is created with a 2D technique, maintaining the same attention to extremely elaborate and accurately detailed sets.

Seven years later, a third episode starring the little hero was produced – *Kirikou et les Hommes et les Femmes* (*Kirikou and the Men and the Women*) – directed entirely by Ocelot. At the time of the movie's release in 2012, the filmmaker already had five feature films under his belt. Also, because of this, he was able to work exclusively in Paris, at the Mac Guff Ligne studio, with a team he had already collaborated with on *Azur & Asmar* in 2006 and *Les Contes de la Nuit* in 2011. Produced on a budget of 7 million euros, the new film's revenue exceeded expectations, with more than one million total admissions. Based on the same principle of *Kirikou et les Bêtes Sauvages*, *Kirikou et les Hommes et les Femmes* brings together five independent adventures. In the stories, we find some familiar characters, such as the mother, the strong woman, and the grumpy old man, but new ones are also introduced. The stories were created through an anomalous creative process. The producers asked a number of screenwriters to propose ideas to develop, specifying that Ocelot would be exclusively responsible for writing the script and dialogues himself. Some fifty synopses of stories were proposed, and of these, five were retained. Bénédicte Galup, very active in Kirikou's first film and co-director of the second one proposed the first three subjects of the five short stories. The first features the strong woman who is helped by Kirikou and his mother following the burning of her hut. In the second, the child helps the grumpy old man in the village, who is threatened by a fierce beast. In the third, Kirikou befriends a character from a distant land, despite the discrimination of the other villagers. Susie Morgenstern, Ocelot's friend and great author of children's literature, had the idea for the episode involving the Griotte. The fifth story, in which Kirikou deals with a flute, was created starting from an idea by Cendrine Maubourguet. The infant is such a talented musician that even the sorceress eventually joins in the dancing.

The Griotte, is a character who simultaneously pays homage to a fundamental figure in West African countries and recalls the director's creative process. The *griots*, or in the feminine, *griottes*, are wandering poets or singers who are responsible for preserving and disseminating the oral tradition of the ancestors. It is a craft that can be practised indiscriminately by both men and women and is transmitted from father to son or at least within the same family. The knowledge of a *griot* or *griotte* ranges from history, literature, epics, mythology, and cosmogony, and their repertoires vary according to the context and culture in which they are formed. Traditional musical instruments such as the kora, bafalon, or djembe are used to complement the narrative. The main purpose of storytelling is to convey moral lessons through the telling of exemplary episodes. Very often griots and griottes are elders, considered authoritative teachers of life because of the many experiences they have collected over the years.[58] The Griotte episode thus gives us insight into a cross-section of traditional West African daily life. As depicted in the film, the stories are normally told in the evening, often on full-moon nights, around a fire where adults and children gather together. The tale makes use of some fixed formulas; as shown in the film, the Griotte converses with the hearers through phrases repeated throughout the fable with the intention of engaging and imprinting messages in the listener's memory (Figure 3.12).

Besides providing us with an intensely appealing account of a pivotal aspect of African culture, the episode underscores the importance of narrative practice more broadly. It also highlights a transfer of knowledge from the old to the new generations, underscored by the clever intervention of Kirikou, whom the wise elder identifies as a possible future griot. Ocelot has often described himself as a storyteller and through the inclusion of this character he seems to remind us of the importance of keeping the memory of past stories alive while at the same time creating new ones. The tale becomes a tool with multiple functions, educational, entertaining, creative, and socially cohesive. In creating the character of the Griotte, Ocelot was inspired in part by the figure of Kirikou's elderly grandfather, but at the same time by the features of French architect and interior designer Andree Putman. The Griotte was meant to represent the wisdom of Africa, its traditions and stories. At the same time,

FIGURE 3.12 La Griotte. *Kirikou et les Hommes et les Femmes*, 2012.
© Ocelot-Studio O.

the director wanted her to appear as an old woman who doesn't
worry about old age and doesn't feel the weight of her years. The
other stories, as is often the case in the director's work, communicate ethical messages such as the importance of generosity
and helping others in need; the acceptance of diversity; the
positive role of art and music.

Although the visual appearance of the production does not
particularly differ from the previous two films, in this case, the
images were made entirely in CGI. It kept the basic image, a
good line drawing and flat colours, to stay true to the aesthetics
of the first film. *Kirikou et les Hommes et les Femmes* was the
third work that Ocelot created digitally, and again he wanted to

maintain a pleasingly artificial look, considered more poetic than a bland hyperrealist digital look. The working process changed considerably, though, facilitating the actual animation phases, since it was possible to make more movements, to develop the characters in more directions, and to have them move more slowly. The design is the result of extensive work by Mac Guff's crew of artists and technicians. Ocelot was responsible for outlining the characters by drawing them freehand and making the models – their front, three-quarter, profile, and back appearance. Once the character models were ready, they were handed over to the crew of modellers. They created a 3D puppet that perfectly matched the initial design. These models were inserted into the sets prepared by the Les Armateurs crew and then developed through three stages of intervention. Firstly, automatic tracing by computer was generated from the volumes of the 3D puppet. This tracking would transform based on the character's position. Afterwards, the subtleties of some movements were drawn with digital tools, such as when a shape failed to generate automatic lines. Finally, careful proofreading was done, with hand touch-ups to improve the details. The main goal was to produce a contour line that behaved logically during the movements and developments of the characters, since the thick contour lines were the most relevant aspect of the film's aesthetic. As reported by Jacque Bled, founder of Mac Guff Ligne, the crew had to eliminate physical logic to achieve a fully satisfactory result graphically.

Unlike the custom of most productions, Ocelot chose, as he always did whenever possible in his films, to record dialogue before the animation was implemented. In addition, the director recorded a voice track acted by him to suggest to the actors the intentions and nuances he sought. During the recording he tried as much as possible to have the voice actors converge at the same time so that they could dialogue directly, ensuring a better rendering of the interactions. The director had a habit of not meeting the actors directly before he chose them for their voices, so as not to be influenced by their appearance or impressions after being introduced to them in person. The music was written by a budding French-Ghanaian musician, Thibault Agyeman. He was chosen following auditions in which musicians were asked to set to music a short piece from the movie. The tryout concerned the film's final scene, in which Kirikou has a flute that can play only four notes – a difficult task that earned Agyeman the part. The young musician took inspiration from the atmosphere of the previous two films. He initially had to familiarise himself with Mandingue folk music, of which he had little knowledge. It was from this genre, the typical accompaniment of griots and griottes, that both Youssou N'Dour and Manu Dibango had drawn for their previous soundtracks. Thibault Agyeman tried to create continuity with these, also adding his own colour to match the different tones of the narrative. The collaboration with the director was deep and ongoing, achieving excellent results, with superb and captivating music.

NOTES

1. For further information refer to ASIFA's official website.
2. Oury, Antoine. "Kirikou et la Sorcière, d'après les contes africains recueillis par François-Victor Équilbecq", in *Actualité*, June 8, 2017.
3. For further information refer to: Asante, Molefi Kete; Abu S. Abarry. *African Intellectual Heritage: A Book of Sources.* Philadelphia: Temple University Press, 1996.
4. Vogler, Christopher. *Il viaggio dell'Eroe: La struttura del mito ad uso di scrittori di narrativa e di cinema.* Roma: Dino Audino, 2020.
5. Ciment, Gilles. "Kirikou et la Sorcière de Michel Ocelot", in *Positif* n. 455, January 1999.
6. Interview by Giannalberto Bendazzi on the occasion of the 11th edition of AniFest, Teplice, Czech Republic, April 26 - May 1, 2012.
7. *Portrait de Michel Ocelot.* Documentary by Véronique Martin, France, 2006.

8. Ocelot, Michel. *Tout sur Kirikou*. Paris: Seuil, 2003, p. 17.
9. Schaëffner, Yves. "Kirikou ou l'innocence récompensée", in Ciné-Bulles n. 184, April, 2000.
10. Neupert, Richard. *French Animation History*, p. 130.
11. Ocelot, Michel, *op. cit.*, p. 79.
12. Ocelot, Michel, *op. cit.*, p. 92.
13. Personal communication with Bénédicte Galup, March 9, 2023.
14. Ocelot, Michel, *op. cit.*, p. 93.
15. Personal communication with Bénédicte Galup, March 9, 2023.
16. "Kirikou et la Sorcière. Dossier de presse." Les Armateurs.
17. Mitchell, Elvis. "Can-Do African Boy Wins and Evil Sorceress Loses", in *The New York Times*, February 18, 2000.
18. Commin, Jean-Paul; Ganne, Valérie; Brunner, Didier. *op. cit.*, p. 21.
19. Neupert, Richard. *French Animation History*, p. 115.
20. Ibid.
21. Bendazzi, Giannalberto. *Animation: A World History*. Boca Raton, FL: CRC Press, Taylor & Francis Group, 2016.
22. Commin, Jean-Paul; Ganne, Valérie; Brunner, Didier. *op. cit.*, p. 27.
23. Ocelot, Michel, *op. cit.*, p. 23.
24. Griseri, Carlo. "Intervista al regista francese Michel Ocelot", in *Cinemaitaliano.info*, December 15, 2012.
25. "Rencontre avec Michel Ocelot (Créateur de Kirikou)". Africa N°1.
26. Neupert, Richard. *French Animation History*, p. 132.
27. In both cases, however, it is not insignificant to mention how these two industries rely, particularly in France, on the production of animated series for television, and only to a lesser extent on the production of animated films for the silver screen.
28. Featherstone, Mike. *Undoing Culture: Globalization, Postmodernism and Identity*. New York: SAGE Publications Ltd, 1995, p. 13.
29. Interview by Giannalberto Bendazzi on the occasion of the 11th edition of AniFest, Teplice, Czech Republic, April 26 - May 1, 2012.
30. Mandelbaum, Jacques. "L'enfant sauvage et la beauté du mal", in *Le Monde*, December 10, 1998.
31. Master-Class by Michel Ocelot moderated by Vanessa Tonnini on the occasion of Movie Up 2020, October 27, 2018.
32. Mury, Cécile. "Le gamin déluré enthousiasme l'Afrique", in *Télérama* n. 2885 April 30, 2005.
33. Ibid.

34. James, Alison. "Some Nix Kirikou Due to Nudity", in *Variety*, December 26, 2005.
35. "Interview dessinée. Michel Ocelot". Interview by FM-Institut français du Maroc, 2019.
36. Neupert, Richard. *French Animation History*, p. 129.
37. Russell, Jamie. "Kirikou and the Sorceress", in *BBC*, June 23, 2003.
38. Ocelot, Michel, *op. cit.*, p. 162.
39. Cormon,Véronique. *Viol et renaissance*. L'Archipel, 2004.
40. Boisseau, Rosita. "Kirikou, sur scène plus vrai que nature", in *Télérama*, October 10, 2007.
41. "Abd Al Malik parle du dessin animé Kirikou". Interview by Brut in occasion of the Festival Lumière, 2018.
42. Cassiau-Haurie, Christophe. "Enfants de Kirikou. Quand les dessinateurs africains font leur cinéma", in *Africultures*, April 1, 2005.
43. Mury, Cécile, "Le gamin déluré enthousiasme l'Afrique", in *Télérama* n. 2885 April 30, 2005.
44. Ibid.
45. "Kabongo le Griot, Studio Pictoon". Interview to Pierre Sauvalle by Pour Une Meilleur Afrik, 2015.
46. Ibid.
47. Mtshali, Seni. *Colonial Stereotypes: Kirikou and the Sorceress as Representation of French views of West Africa*, University of Witwatersrand, Johannesburg, 2012.
48. "Abd Al Malik parle du dessin animé Kirikou". Interview by Brut in occasion of the Festival Lumière, 2018.
49. "Interview dessinée. Michel Ocelot". Interview by FM-Institut français du Maroc, 2019.
50. Ibid.
51. Rosaldo, Renato. "Ideology, Place, and People without Culture", in *Place and Voice in Anthropological Theory*, Vol. 3, No. 1, February 1988, p. 78.
52. Ngom, Abdou. "Postcolonial Studies: An Avenue to Examining Africa's Indigenous Knowledge Systems" in *Africology: The Journal of Pan African Studies*, vol.11, no.1, December 2017, pp. 272–290.
53. Ngom, Abdou, *op. cit.*, p. 274.
54. Commin, Jean-Paul; Ganne, Valérie; Brunner, Didier., *op. cit.*, p. 44.
55. Personal communication with Bénédicte Galup, March 9, 2023.

56. Labesse, Patrick. "Manu Dibango meets Kirikou. France's Hot New Film Soundtrack", in *RFI Musique*, December 27, 2005.
57. Commin, Jean-Paul; Ganne, Valérie; Brunner, Didier., *op. cit.*, p. 48.
58. Baker, Rob; Ellen Draper. "If One Thing Stands, Another Will Stand Beside It: An Interview with Chinua Achebe", in *Parabola* 173, Fall 1992, pp. 19–27.

CHAPTER 4

A Beautiful Stranger

Azur & Asmar

A NEW MEDIUM FOR A NEW STORY

During the period Michel Ocelot was constantly travelling to promote his first feature film, *Kirikou et la Sorcière*, he began to develop the subject of his next production, *Azur et Asmar* (*Azur & Asmar - The Princes' Quest - 2006*). Visiting many different countries and cities in a few months the author began to reflect on the conflicting relationships between nations and peoples, rooted in history and consolidated by tradition. He began to reflect on a story that could investigate the reasons for hostility between people belonging to apparently opposite and conflicting worlds. Likewise, he wanted to demonstrate the potential to overcome these seemingly insurmountable differences. After reasoning upon several options – including a story that staged the ancient rivalry between France and Germany and a tale set in imaginary countries with completely invented languages – Ocelot thought about the relationship between France and Maghreb. In the course of his travelling he couldn't help but notice how intolerable the climate of hostility in Europe towards those considered foreigners and strangers was becoming. The

DOI: 10.1201/9781003292173-5

author, therefore, decided to construct a story that could overturn commonplaces and recurring stereotypes.

Azur & Asmar is set partly in medieval Europe and partly in an unidentified Arab-speaking North African country. The film transports the viewer to a fascinating and shimmering medieval world that oscillates between Europe and North Africa, between European and Arab Islamic culture. This allowed the director to "celebrate the brilliant Islamic civilisation of the Middle Ages"[1] and to unravel a plot of inter-country relations, as Maghreb and France had been historically linked for many centuries. He could also gracefully stage in the form of a fable what he described as "ordinary animosity between born and recent citizens".[2] We follow the story of two kids, with seemingly opposite traits. The contrast is already evident in the two names Azur, meaning light blue in French, and Asmar, a personal name derived from the Arabic word "asmar", meaning "brown" or "dark-skinned". The two protagonists are raised together in a castle by Asmar's mother, Jénane. The woman is in the service of Azur's father as the child's nursemaid. Jénane and Asmar are foreigners and she speaks to both of them in French and Arabic, treating them equally and narrating to them the Djinn Fairy folktale. After their early childhood is spent in close contact, the two children are separated by Azur's father, who decides to chase Jénane and his son away. Azur, once a young adult, decides to cross the sea to reach the country on the opposite coast, in search of the Djinn Fairy. Initially, Azur finds himself in a very unfavourable situation. He discovers that his blue eyes are considered evil because of superstitious beliefs; the young man is shunned badly by the locals. Azur starts to despise the unknown country so much that he closes his eyes, vowing never to open them again so as not to see all that ugliness and evil. A beggar named Crapoux, also a French speaking foreigner, but long established there, helps Azur get his bearings. He leads him to Jénane, who in the meantime has become a rich merchant. Thanks to the generosity of Jénane, who welcomes him with open arms, Azur begins to discover and appreciate the country wonders. In Jénane house Azur meets again Asmar, who is now hostile to him, mindful of the injustices suffered by Azur's father. Both set off in search of the Djinn fairy, aided by some positive and wise characters, including the little girl princess Chamsous Sabah. Initially, in competition, the two protagonists ultimately are able to overcome their conflicts to reunite brotherly and succeed in their quest (Figure 4.1).

The feature film plot plays on the contrast, rich in details and aesthetic cues, between these two antithetical figures. One poor, the other rich. One foreigner, the other native. In the course of the story the protagonists swap roles to show, through a change of perspective, the difficulties of those who migrate. The concept was familiar to Ocelot. He had experienced feelings of disorientation and dismay when he was moved with his parents to France, after his childhood in Guinea. In addition to these insights, the filmmaker was particularly struck by a story he heard on the radio. An Englishman had found his childhood nanny in Lebanon after several years and completely by chance. Hearing about this reunion moved Ocelot deeply, thus he took inspiration from it for his screenplay. As usual, the filmmaker wrote the story in his own hand. The characters were all born from Ocelot's pencil in the quietness and solitude of his Parisian home. In moments of intense creation, the director transformed the rooms of his house into a studio. The sliding doors were flipped over and used as a desk until the work was completed. In this improvised studio, the beginnings of the project took place: The creation of the script, which Ocelot wrote in just two weeks, followed by a full immersion in drawing to begin sketching the characters, strictly working, without music or coffee. Once he completed what could be accomplished directly at home, the doors returned to their place as if by magic. Before contacting producers or distributors, he made sure to be at a stage close to completion. "I'm the one who writes, I'm the one who decides, I do what I want. In fact, I don't ask; I write, I rewrite, and when I feel it's not bad, I really want to have it read, for example, to a

FIGURE 4.1 *Azur & Asmar.* CGI animation, 2006. © Nord-Ouest Production / Mac Guff Ligne / Studio O / France 3 Cinéma / Rhône-Alpes Cinéma / Artémis Production / Zahorimédia / Intuition Films / Lucky Red.

producer I'm interested in",[3] he declared. For most of his movies, he followed this procedure.

After sketching out the main plot lines, he worked on the *scenarimage*, which was completed in about a year. During this phase, he called together his most trusted collaborators as soon as possible (Figure 4.2).

Approximately one hundred characters would be clearly visible on the screen as well as two hundred extras, all to be drawn. Ocelot was in charge of the main characters whilst the collaborators were responsible for the concept and design of the secondary figures. Along with a restricted team of six to eight designers, he began the work of documenting and creating characters and sets. At this stage, the team worked closely together in Ocelot's apartment and spent a lot of time with each other, like a small family, benefiting from plenty of time and creative freedom. Such a small crew was quite uncommon in animated feature film productions. The filmmaker wanted to maintain the informal atmosphere of mutual esteem that he had experienced in previous, more improvised productions.

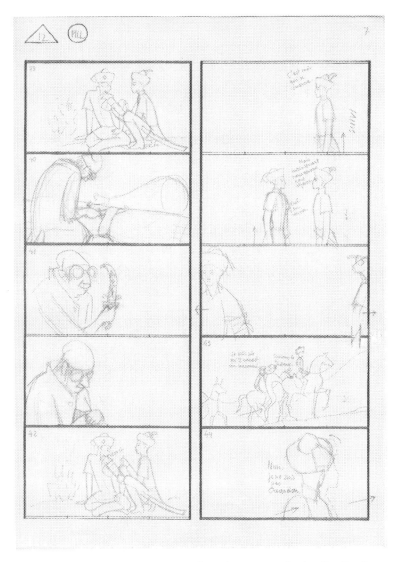

FIGURE 4.2   *Azur & Asmar*. Storyboard, 2006. © Ocelot-Studio O.

Anne-Lise Koehler and Eric Serre assisted him in the more demanding aspects of production. They were the first to be contacted, in June 2001, when the work was only a rough draft. Eric Serre took care of the secondary characters: The riding teacher, the dancing teacher, the tutor, the coachman, the characters that made up the crowd, the villains, the merchants, and the soldiers. As Ocelot and Serre knew each other and had already worked together on *Kirikou et la Sorcière*, the director left to his aide considerable wiggle room in the creative process. Serre was also entrusted with the coordination and supervision of the drawing team, which created a total of approximately thirteen thousand drawings. Under the constant supervision of the director, Serre set up the layouts for every shot – one thousand two hundred and eighty in total. The production of a layout consisted of a fairly accurate indication to be given to those who would enact animation and assembly in post-production. The preparatory work done by the team was to outline the setting, the angles and framing of the scenes, the main positions of the characters in the picture, dialogue, camera movements, and duration of the scene. The scenery was separated into several levels to create a multilevel effect of depth. In the background was the sketch of the set. Drawn separately were the various characters, props, and other elements, to be organised on different distinct planes to suggest a certain position in space. In this graphic setting, 3D animation was then implemented. Serre explained it as follows:

> This work is repeated for each shot of the film. To give a precise example, let us imagine a side shot in which we see palm trees in the foreground, characters in the background and other palm trees in the background, on several levels. The precise description of the action of the shot can be found in Michel's small storyboard sketch. [...] I isolate the different layers on different perforated sheets. They are made of very thin white paper. You can stack several sheets on a light table to see all the drawings in transparency. Then, to return to the foreground elements, each element that will move independently of the others during the tracking shot is drawn on a

separate sheet. Say for example a layer of palm tree trunks, then a layer of foliage, then more trunks. Then there will be a white sheet representing the layer on which the characters will move, and then the different leaves that correspond to the trees in the background. […] At the end, the final set and animation are brought together to check that everything works[4] (Figures 4.3 and 4.4).

As had already been the case for *Kirikou et la Sorcière*, Anne-Lise Koehler worked on the set designs and on the ideation of the animals. Besides being a talented draughtswoman Koehler was a skilled sculptor of animals made from wire and paper, so this task was particularly suitable for her. The very first figure Koehler designed was the bird Saïmourh, which she began to conceive while driven by enthusiasm for the new project. She recalled:

> I was getting impatient waiting for the film to start and I said to Michel Ocelot, 'Come on, we have to start! I'll come and work at yours!' And there I drew the Saïmourh bird, inspired by its representation in various Persian miniatures.[5]

Koehler had already exhibited her brilliance in her excellent work for Ocelot's first feature film, but in this case, her involvement was further stimulated by personal interest. The creation of sets was a particularly motivating and exciting task as she had spent part of her childhood in Morocco. The work of studying, documenting, and creating the sceneries was therefore a way of deepening the visual culture of a place that had helped shape her tastes and aesthetic sense. In addition to defining atmospheres, graphic conception of environments and details useful for the narrative, Koehler was also responsible for coordinating the team of set designers and colourists. The work

FIGURE 4.3 Azur and Princess Chamsous Sabah at the palace. 3D layout and drawing. *Azur & Asmar*, 2006. © Ocelot-Studio O / Nord-Ouest Production.

FIGURE 4.4 Azur and Princess Chamsous Sabah at the palace. Placement of the characters in the digital set. *Azur & Asmar*, 2006. © Nord-Ouest Production / Mac Guff Ligne / Studio O / France 3 Cinéma / Rhône-Alpes Cinéma / Artémis Production / Zahorimédia / Intuition Films / Lucky Red.

was divided among all the professionals without predetermined hierarchies, but entrusting tasks to each one according to their specific inclinations and talents.

Ocelot demanded historical and geographical accuracy. Both of the countries represented, the European one and the North African one, are fictional places, two imaginary contexts where special effort is directed to the creation of a fable-like, but also credible, environment. Therefore, the creative process was accompanied by preliminary studies and the consulting of many books and computer sources. The director himself read numerous books, including the Koran and the Gospels. He also visited the three Maghreb countries – Algeria, Morocco, and Tunisia – with camera in hand, to bring back as faithful a memory as possible. He went to Algiers, where he visited Bastion 23, which is an example of Ottoman architecture in Algeria, and the Bardo National Museum in Tunis. These two places inspired him to create a beautiful Moorish house. At the Bardo Museum, he was inspired by a very tall hairstyle, made of metal, to create the headdress of one of his characters, the Djinn Fairy.[6] Work proceeded, but not without setbacks; the filmmaker recounted how much he had admired the decorative potential of prickly pears, present in every corner in the Maghreb towns he had visited. He included a large number of them in his sets. However, he only realised later that these plants were introduced to North Africa only after the colonisation of the Americas. To his great regret, he had to remove them! This anecdote shows how documentary accuracy was a key element to be respected during the creative process. Although the story would be a fairytale, it was essential to depict a credible, reliable setting; adhering to reality and history. Inspiration was taken from Maghrebi and Andalusian architecture and monuments, as well as architectural masterpieces from the areas of the former Ottoman Empire. The Djinn Fairy's palace at the end of the film takes its inspiration from the magnificent Blue Mosque in Istanbul.

Koehler recounted how they always started from real architecture and then made some modifications. One example is the

FIGURE 4.5 Jénane's garden. *Azur & Asmar*, CGI animation, 2006. © Nord-Ouest Production / Mac Guff Ligne / Studio O / France 3 Cinéma / Rhône-Alpes Cinéma / Artémis Production / Zahorimédia / Intuition Films / Lucky Red.

garden of Jénane's house, where the spaces are inspired by the Alhambra in Granada, whilst the roofs and arches were created by combining different features of existing structures with fictitious elements (Figure 4.5).

Scenography and framing were organised around strong vertical and horizontal lines, ensuring an effect of order and formal organisation that was instrumental in avoiding interference with the audience's understanding of the story. Similar choices were made to those that had already been experimented with successfully in the silhouette films. Simple framing and very limited camera movements. First and foremost, the director wanted to communicate with the audience, to move them; thus the elaborate hypertrophic decorations never masked the clarity, simplicity, and symmetry on which the shots were based. The props were also created with immense care, in many cases reproduced in three dimensions before being drawn and placed in the context of the set design. Everything was crafted with great precision while the director supervised with an exigent, yet passionate and cheerful eye. The convivial atmosphere allowed everyone to develop their talents and dwell on the details without feeling under pressure. Recounted Koehler:

> I remember a cake that Juliette Nardin, one of the set designers, had to draw. She was so busy with her work that she baked one to make sure she got it right. Not only did she make a beautiful design, but afterwards we could enjoy eating the model!

Once the first phase of work was completed – carried out with this small group of collaborators and lasting two years – they moved on from Ocelot's apartment to work at MacGuff Ligne studio. The studio, which had specialised in digital animation since the 1980s, is currently one of the largest and most prestigious in France. The filmmaker chose MacGuff not only because they appeared to do a wonderful job, but also because, after observing them in action, he thought they would get along well. Indeed they did. At the time MacGuff was already one of the best French studios specialising in computer animation and Ocelot no longer had to worry about budget constraints. *Azur & Asmar* was his most expensive film, costing a total of 10 million euros. The filmmaker had finally emerged from the uncertainty of previous years and enjoyed great confidence from investors, following the astounding success of *Kirikou et la Sorcière*. Nonetheless, he remained true to his values, without subordinating aesthetic and narrative refinement to commercial success. As Eric Serre recalled, "Working on Azur & Asmar gave us the impression that we were making a work of art, like rebels escaping the usual production system, and not an animated film!"[7]

At MacGuff, the small team of close collaborators was flanked by a crew of about thirty people specialising in digital animation. They were divided into small teams, with a few people responsible for a specific area, whether it was animation, rendering, or lighting. It was a fairly classic organisational pipeline, where the director always had the last word. The result was superb work that combined ornamental richness and simplicity. Ocelot aimed for beauty and perfection:

> For the first and last time in my life, I had the right to do luxury. And it was an extreme pleasure. One of the first luxuries was having everyone around me and not making the film in five different countries […]. The other luxury was to have enough money to allow me to […] make the beautiful […] without having limitations".[8]

It took about eighteen months for the creation of the sets, the digital modelling of the characters, and the actual animation. Added to this were several months of work to implement post-production. Already in the days of *Kirikou*, Ocelot had made the most of the potential of new computer-based technologies, and on this occasion, too, he decided to use the newest techniques on the market.

He chose to use computer graphics for their enormous potential, and, in fact, the technique permitted him to intervene in errors and afterthoughts while avoiding some of the slow pace typical of cel animation. CGI did not affect the director's aesthetic choices; on the contrary, the tool was adapted to achieve the effects of poetic simplicity and purity. Many of the scenes play on the juxtaposition of highly stylised figures against extremely elaborate backgrounds. The richness of the ornaments typical of medieval Islamic architecture was exploited to its full potential, but avoiding weighing down the narrative or over-shadowing the characters. CGI allowed the creation of hyper-realistic embroideries and jewels that would have been unaffordable with cel animation. The director and his crew enjoyed the possibility to experiment with volumes and details. Whilst the bodies were reduced to flat surfaces, the faces were

FIGURE 4.6 Jénane. *Azur & Asmar.* CGI Animation, 2006. © Nord-Ouest Production / Mac Guff Ligne / Studio O / France 3 Cinéma / Rhône-Alpes Cinéma / Artémis Production / Zahorimédia / Intuition Films / Lucky Red.

modelled as beautiful sculptures, as was the jewellery, inspired by fine Berber craftsmanship. Earrings, necklaces, and other ornaments were designed and recreated with exactness and elegance, with a rich, sparkling visual effect (Figure 4.6).

The new technique, furthermore, allowed Ocelot to play with a large number of characters and extras, creating complex scenes and calibrating movements carefully. Digital animation enabled control of even the slowest and most articulated movements, since, contrary to what one might think, it is the slowest movements that are the most difficult to animate, precisely because in slowness the error is more visibly traceable.

The costumes of the extras were based on contemporary Moroccan clothing. Those of Azur and Asmar were developed from examples found in fifteenth-century Persian miniatures. He also drew on European painting, borrowing from Flemish artists such as Van Eyck, Nicolas Fouquet, and from medieval French sources such as the fifteenth-century French illuminated codex *Très Riches Heures du Duc de Berry*. The folds of the garments were removed from all fabrics, resulting in a flat and uniform final effect that was inspired by the sharpness of 1920s and 1930s graphics. The elimination of folds and shadows facilitated the animation of the characters, but it was primarily a precise aesthetic choice, guaranteeing clarity and synthetism. There is also an evenly diffused frontal application of lighting that contributes a touch of unreality to the figures, an approach reminiscent of the abstract light of some Italian Renaissance artists, most notably Piero della Francesca. Such lighting reveals a vision of the world represented as a harmonious, orderly spectacle. The director contrasted the anthropomorphic hyperrealism of the big US studios such as Disney, Pixar, and DreamWorks with a fabulous anti-realism, with rich sets and costumes that recaptured the flavour of fairytale illustrations. As Ocelot declared:

> I don't want to do realistic 3D, like the Americans usually do. [...] I'm not interested in that at all, like realistic lighting, reflections of reflections [...] I always want to keep it light; I am a storyteller and I play with the audience. I want them to be intelligent with me, to invent with me. I don't want my images to be pre-chewed, over-chewed. The audience has to chew a little.[9]

On the advice of Jacques Bled, founder and CEO of MacGuff Ligne, Ocelot contacted producer Christophe Rossignon, co-founder of Nord-Ouest production company, together with Philip Boëffard. The producer felt very honoured by this choice, but above all surprised, as Nord-Ouest had produced only live-action cinema up to that point. *Azur & Asmar*'s story intrigued and engaged him from the start, convincing him to take on this new challenge. Rossignon considered the story "accessible to children and adults alike, as Michel has within him the capacity to wonder". That would be the beginning of a long and fruitful collaboration. The movie was the result of a co-production between France, Belgium, Italy, and Spain. Released in French cinemas in October 2006, *Azur & Asmar* was distributed in France by Diaphana Distribution. The first screening of the movie was at the Cannes Film Festival during the Directors' Fortnight in 2006, where it was greeted with an excellent response. The feature film was warmly received at animation festivals, it was honoured with several awards and sold one and a half million tickets in France.[10] Ocelot by then occupied an illustrious position in the world of animated cinema. His previous works had been critically acclaimed and loved by audiences. With *Azur & Asmar* the director confirmed his status as one of the leading figures in French and international animated pictures.

THE REPRESENTATION OF ALTERITY

Despite being set in the Middle Ages, *Azur & Asmar* is a film that intended to narrate the present through the coded language of the fairy tale. In the years prior to the feature film's release, there was a great deal of attention focused on the migration phenomenon: Europe saw a resurgence of racism and xenophobia, particularly towards people of Arab descent, even if they were citizens of European countries or had been resident in Europe for several years. Ocelot reported in many interviews his concern about this hostility, especially since, living in Paris, his daily life took place in a city he perceived with pleasure as cosmopolitan and multicultural. In such a climate of discord, the film was meant to be a message of hope and brotherhood. Immediately came the confirmation the direction taken was right. The small group assisting the author in the early stages of the film had only started drawing a handful of days before when they witnessed the 9/11 attacks on television. The team stopped working for a few days, but after the initial daze, they resumed drawing with renewed enthusiasm. The subject was suited to dealing with relevant topical issues. They felt the movie had become indispensable.

The entire concept of the film is aimed at depicting dialogue between cultures, and the emphasis on multiculturalism as the founding pillar of the entire production was also placed in the movie's end credits, accompanied by a message highlighting the twenty-five nationalities represented in the cast and crew. The subject and the screenplay, however, are the work of Ocelot himself, therefore it is worth questioning to what extent a European author can legitimately represent a culture that is not his own. It is useful to point out how Ocelot uses symmetry and binarism as foundations upon which he develops his story. Such East/West binarism has in itself problematic roots in that it takes its starting point from an opposition that is the result of an inherently colonial mentality. Indeed, it derives from the discursive construction of the concept of "Orient", the impact of which was first theorised by Edward Said in his 1978 essay "Orientalism". Said defined Orientalism as the set of institutions created by the West, useful for establishing relations of force and control with the "Orient". This took place through political, economic, and military practices and cultural concepts, which constructed a system of notions and meanings related to it. Visual culture also played a major role, insofar as Western Orientalist imagery was bolstered by the paintings of eighteenth- and nineteenth-century European artists. However, while the film starts from this conceptually problematic foundation, and the presence of some biased ideas can be detected, Ocelot's effort to subvert conceptions normally associated with the East is significant. In fact, if the West has always been connected with positive ideas such as "modern, civilized, and productive", the East has been related to notions of the opposite.[11] *Azur & Asmar* aims to make evident the concept of "otherness", however, by questioning the preconceived basis with which the Other is associated.

With the usual didactic concern, the French animator conceived a plot that would reverse the concept of "otherness" and the standard depiction of the migration experience. Everything unfolds through a reversal device designed to exchange roles and positions between the two protagonists in the course of the story. In the first part of the film Asmar and his mother Jénane are strangers in a foreign land. They are poor, whilst Azur is the son of the wealthy local lord. Upon reaching the other side of the sea, Azur sees his condition reversed. Caught in a storm, he is shipwrecked on unknown shores and finds himself stripped of all possessions, poor and disoriented in a country that rejects him. He finds himself in the role of the migrant. Such reversal is a particularly effective device in the narrative, aimed at stimulating the viewer's identification with the character. The filmmaker stated he identified with the character of Azur and simultaneously with Crapoux, the two European characters, guests in the Maghrebi country. Crapoux in particular was often mentioned by the filmmaker as a representation of himself in the aftermath of his return to France. Unable to adapt, young Michel had in fact rejected for years the new French city in which he lived, denying himself the pleasure of living in a theretofore unfamiliar place. It is arguable that the director had a Western audience in mind as he conceived the script or, at the very least, shaped it following his own life experience. In fact, among the negative critical reviews regarding the film, the most common objection is over whether Azur is the one leading most of the action in the movie,[12] and some commentators have pointed out that Azur's prominence tends to overshadow Asmar,[13] with traits of white saviorism.[14] Nevertheless, the complex interrelationship between the various characters and his disadvantaged condition at many stages complicates Azur's leading role.

A very convincing reading of the animated feature was proposed by Fotini Apostolou in the article "Cultural Translations: Transcending Boundaries in Michel Ocelot's Animated Film Azur & Asmar". Apostolou argued that the film "embarks on a transcendence of all types of boundaries, a perpetual translation or transportation between the two cultures, [...] thus promoting their complementarity".[15] Throughout the film we witness a perpetual crossing of borders, bringing attention to the space "in between", which emerges in the relationship between the two countries' respective cultures. Indeed, the film's characters are united by a common absence of homeland, their cross-cultural identity, and the ability to shift between one culture and another, between one language and another, with familiarity. Apostolou argued that everything in the feature film universe is meant to disorient the viewers and overturn their preconceived notions. She emphasised the crucial importance of the first scene, in which Jénane breastfeeds the two children and simultaneously communicates with them in a mixture of Arabic and French. This upheaval of the "dominant patriarchal rule" carries with it a restatement of oral culture, as opposed to the "prevalent written culture".[16] This establishes a connection with orality related to the Arab tradition, whereby stories are passed from generation to generation through speech. Azur's father, who embodies an omnipresent political power, recognises in this passage of knowledge a menace to colonisation. When Azur reveals he wants to cross the sea to reach his nurse's country, his father attributes this choice to the woman's negative influence. Azur has been contaminated by another culture, and, fascinated by it, decides to embark on a journey of discovery. It can be agreed with Richard Neupert, who finds this metaphor a replication of European stereotypes, presenting a revisited Orientalism that identifies the East as a matriarchal land that offers great promise to Azur, the sensitive, non-colonialist, European.[17] However, Apostolou noted that Azur arrives in the Maghrebi country, prior to French colonisation, yet he doesn't have the appearance of a coloniser: "He is there, rather, as the 'colonised' Other, who has already been conquered by the culture of the distant Other, which is an imaginary Motherland for him to which he has to return".[18] After the shipwreck, devoid of all he had, the boy is deprived of his former identity and identified as evil and dangerous. The viewer is then led to identify with the unpleasant and feared migrant. By the time of his encounter with Asmar, the reversal of roles is evident. Asmar has become a handsome and wealthy young man and refuses to turn to his "brother", reinforcing Azur's exclusion.

Apostolou posed the question: "Who is Azur? Does he stand for the Self in the Self/Other dichotomy?". She believes that the answer to this question is negative, stating that Azur:

> was brought up as the son of alien 'mother' and a native father, he stands in a liminal space, neither here nor there; he does have white skin, but his upbringing identifies him with the dark continent. […] His existence, therefore […] is even more marginal than that of his dark-skinned 'brother', Asmar, who can partly identify with his native culture and language.[19]

On the contrary, Azur's belonging lies in a hybrid space between the two cultures. Ocelot is not free of bias, but he succeeds in his intent since, as conceptualised by Homi Bhabha in his book *The Location of Culture*, it is precisely in this liminal space, this space "in between" that a path can open up towards the concept of an international culture, and the film *Azur & Asmar* achieves this by operating in a hybrid terrain, establishing contact between Western audiences, to whom the film is directed, and the SWANA (South West Asian and North African) area's culture.

VISUALITY AND SOUND BETWEEN TWO CULTURES

One of the reasons the film should not be considered a mere cultural appropriation, lies in the relationship the director establishes with visual and cultural sources. As aforementioned, the filmmaker spent much of the preparation phase slavishly researching and documenting. The aesthetic research is enriched by a multitude of varied sources with the goal of bringing back an accurate transcription of the historical and cultural context in which the characters move. This did not preclude some artistic licence from being taken. The film ultimately had to fascinate, not show documentary images. As the plot of *Azur & Asmar* was not inspired by any existing fairy tale, it draws partly from the mythology of Arab countries. In the course of the film, several figures with magical powers appear, either invented by the author or adapted from Arab and Muslim traditions. Characters such as the Djinn Fairy or the Scarlet Lion were born from Michel Ocelot's imagination (Figure 4.7).

Furthermore, in the case of the depiction of the Djinns, the director and his team could not draw from figurative sources, as these invisible spirits from pre-Islamic mythology are mentioned in the Koran, but rarely represented.

The effort admirably applied in documentation shelters the film from being completely subservient to the Western Orientalist gaze. In the book *From Orientalism to Postcolonialism: Asia, Europe and the Lineages of Difference*, Sucheta Mazumdar and Vasant Kaiwar pointed out:

> in the framework of Orientalism, there was Europe on the one hand and the 'people without history' on the other. European civilization was unique, self-generated, self-identical, self-propelled; European history could be framed in progressive frames as Ancient, Medieval, Modern. Other civilizations had 'tradition' [...]. European modernity evolved endogenously while in all other cases it had to be induced externally, through the direct agency of the West.[20]

Therefore, the choice to show the Arab Middle Ages has additional value in restoring dignity to the history of a culture largely unknown in the West. The movie thus becomes a tribute to another culture, it is a picture that invites the audience to document and discover countries commonly associated with negative concepts such as fear, barbarism, and backwardness. "I wanted people to realise that the sets were created from real

FIGURE 4.7   The Djinn Fairy. *Azur & Asmar*, 2006. © Ocelot-Studio O.

elements. I wanted to tell people: 'These wonderful places exist: go and see them!'", declared Ocelot.[21]

The depiction of a precise geographical and historical context also places the film in stark contrast to Disney's renowned classic

Aladdin (Ron Clements, John Muskers – 1992). Despite that film's huge commercial success, *Aladdin* was a film at the centre of various critical debates, to the point of being named in 2006 by *Entertainment Weekly* as one of the twenty-five most controversial films of all time.[22] Set in the imaginary city of Agrabah, the Disney film blends architectural features far apart in time and space, drawing indiscriminately from a pool of ideal knowledge driven by superficial cognition and retracing a distinctly Orientalist view. In contrast to a historical depiction anchored in a real time and place, the movie prefers fantasies of an abstract exotic and alien Arabia as a backdrop for a formulaic romance. In two essays collected in the book *The Emperor's Old Groove. Decolonizing Disney's Magic Kingdom*, Christiane Staninger and Christopher Wise pointed out how much the film carried racist and harmful stereotypes, perpetuating an ideological Western view of the East as a place of violence and oppression. *Aladdin* was described as a propaganda film for Western imperialism, as it shows "the supposed unworkability of Middle Eastern traditions and the need for American intervention".[23] In the film, there is a strong contrast between the three leading characters – Aladdin, Jasmine, and the Genie – and the other figures. If most of the characters, including the villain, Jafar, speak with Middle Eastern accent, the three protagonists flaunt distinctly American speech. All three are depicted as suffering from backward laws enacted by a society that oppresses them, and their words and desires for freedom reveal their adherence to Western capitalistic values.[24] Furthermore, Jasmine was modelled to embody the strong and independent young woman, the new ideal of girls in the years of the film's release. However, Jasmine's supposed resourcefulness is a pretext to remark on the superiority of U.S. culture, as her feminist ambitions are Western longings. To make the character appealing, Disney's animators took cues from the fashionable clothing style popular among California teenage girls of the time.[25] Moreover, in addition to being misrepresented, her figure is sexualised as the object of desire contested by two men, Aladdin and Jafar, echoing the Western trope of the exotic and sensual Oriental woman.

Conversely, the two main female figures who appear in *Azur & Asmar* are alien to this characterisation, as Sabina Shah highlighted in her essay "The Portrayal of the Historical Muslim Female on Screen",[26] Jénane and Chamsous Sabah are depicted as two female characters possessing the knowledge and power to manage their own destiny. They are not figures waiting to be rescued, but perfectly in control of their own existence. Jénane is a wealthy merchant, an educated and unprejudiced woman, the repository of the positive values conveyed by the film. Chamsous Sabah is an intelligent and perceptive child to whom Azur turns for advice and guidance. Shah emphasised that young Chamsous Sabah is not at all passive. The little girl undermines the usual cliché of the princess exhibiting an active interest in politics. She tells how she became the heir to the throne, since all the men in her family have been assassinated by enemies, and she repeats that as she is a girl no one is thinking of killing her. When Azur replies that sooner or later her enemies will identify her as a danger she replies that then it will be too late; she will be stronger and have *them* killed. The princess is an extremely fascinating character; she is a strong-willed and nuanced figure, to the point that a journalist suggested she deserved a film entirely dedicated to her[27] (Figure 4.8).

Richard Neupert pointed out how a symbol common to Western Orientalist narratives is preserved in *Azur & Asmar*: The European male who must penetrate the Oriental woman's chamber and metaphorically unveil her before possessing her.[28] Nonetheless, the Djinn Fairy, the character in the most conventional role – the hero's reward for succeeding in the quest – does not passively wait for salvation but chooses to reveal herself by virtue of the talents and kindheartedness shown by the two young men in the feat. According to Shah and Neupert,[29] the trope is further complicated by racial diversity, through the

FIGURE 4.8   Model of Princess Chamsous Sabah. *Azur & Asmar*, 2006.
© Ocelot-Studio O.

mating of Azur with the Djinn Fairy and Asmar with her white European cousin, the Elf Fairy.[30] This pairing also comes about as a result of the Elf Fairy's declaration that first they must get to know each other, converse and then decide, putting part of the agency back into the hands of the girls. Cultural diversity is also shown throughout the course of the story, both in the varied backgrounds and cultural identities of the characters – for instance, the wise old Jewish intellectual – and in the explicit display that numerous places of worship belonging to different religions can coexist in the imaginary North African city. In order to create bridges between cultures, Ocelot chose not to dub the dialogue in Arabic, a sensible choice that lays the groundwork for respecting the culture represented. "There are many languages in the world and no subtitles. I want people to accept this diversity",[31] stated the director. "It was crucial for me that the viewer also experience the plight of the emigrant, the feeling of being lost in front of a foreign and unknown language".[32]

FIGURE 4.9 Princess Chamsous Sabah. *Azur & Asmar.* CGI animation, 2006. © Nord-Ouest Production / Mac Guff Ligne / Studio O / France 3 Cinéma / Rhône-Alpes Cinéma / Artémis Production / Zahorimédia / Intuition Films / Lucky Red.

He also added that he believed it would be an important experience for a child to be able to hear the sound of another language as a not at all strange occurrence, as children are used to not understanding everything perfectly and they are comfortable with that. The filmmaker has repeatedly claimed that the reasons for his success among the youngest can be ascribed to his approach to them. "I've never made films for children. That's why children like my films. Nobody wants to be treated as a baby"[33] (Figure 4.9).

The search for voices to dub the characters followed a long and carefully handled process. Ocelot collaborated with several professionals who could scout out the most suitable people to play the various roles. His inclination was not to call in famous actors and actresses, but simply anyone who would be most appropriate for the part without worrying whether they were complete unknowns. Palestinian actress and film director Hiam Abbas was hired to coordinate the actors performing in Arabic, to supervise whether they could speak the language correctly and if they would be up to the role. When Abbas read the part of

Jénane she was smitten with it and immediately asked the director to give it to her, but Ocelot initially responded negatively. The director didn't like to meet the people who would act for his films, so as not to be influenced by his general impression of them. He, therefore, asked Abbas to continue looking for an actress who could play the central role of the nurse. The search continued for quite some time and ranged beyond French territory, including a casting call organised in Tunis. Eventually, he became convinced that Abbas would be perfect to play Jénane. "I think that what 'blocked' Michel as far as I was concerned was that he absolutely did not want to see the people before hearing their voices",[34] recounted Abbas.

For the composition of the soundtrack, the French animator immediately thought of Gabriel Yared, whom he considered a great film musician, and a great musician tout court. Yared also possessed the ideal profile as he belonged to the two shores of the Mediterranean: France and Lebanon. Ocelot proposed the film to him and, after reading the story, the musician immediately accepted. Yared later reported that he considered *Azur & Asmar* one of the most beautiful animated films he had watched up to that time. The director recounted an amusing anecdote about his first meeting with Yared. The first thing the musician told him was "I have to warn you, I am not interested in pictures and in films". Ocelot was a little taken aback, then answered "I have to warn you, my favourite sound is silence". They became great friends after that.[35] The composer was already very famous at the time, having worked for many successful films and won numerous awards, including an Oscar for the score of the live-action movie *The English Patient*. According to Ocelot:

> We could not afford such a star, but as he liked the story and is a gentleman, he forgot about any Hollywood demands [...] It was still a very expensive affair! Gabriel is used to the best, he had to have two symphonic

orchestras, several choirs, flawless soloists, and mixing at the Abbey Road Studios, of Beatles and Star Wars fame.[36]

The musician worked far in advance of the final stages of production, since some music had to be composed before implementing the animation. In particular, the lullaby that opens the film, as well as the scene in which we see four musicians playing in Jénane's garden. With his usual meticulousness, Ocelot filmed the recording with the musicians in the studio to obtain gesture references to be used to animate the musicians in the film. Yared used instruments common in the music of SWANA areas, such as oud, qanun, or Arabic violins. The rhythmic pattern of these musical traditions comes into play especially in the chase scenes, rhythmically supported by a lute, qanun, and percussion. The composer perfectly illustrated the characters' journey, particularly by frequently echoing the lullaby of the early scenes, performed by the Algerian Berber singer Souad Massi, introducing elements of this melody at other moments of the movie. The lullaby takes on the form of a theme that runs throughout the film until its return at the conclusion. The eventful rhythm punctuates the adventurous journey, and the repetition of the theme translates the idea of the search effectively. In the scenes set in medieval Europe, Yared created an old-fashioned musical commentary, played with the aid of woodwind instruments. The latter returned frequently, along with the brass, in the rest of the soundtrack, creating a very effective cross-cultural blending style. Music thus lends its richness and dramatic quality in further support of the cultural amalgamations that visually run through the film. "When Gabriel's music arrived in my pictures, it was a miracle; everything matched", declared the director[37] (Figure 4.10).

Azur & Asmar was distributed in many European countries including Spain, Greece, Italy, and UK; and non-European countries, including Brazil, Korea, US, and Japan. It also

FIGURE 4.10 *Azur & Asmar*. CGI animation, 2006. © Nord-Ouest Production / Mac Guff Ligne / Studio O / France 3 Cinéma / Rhône-Alpes Cinéma / Artémis Production / Zahorimédia / Intuition Films / Lucky Red.

achieved much success in the SWANA regions. In Lebanon, an exemplary teacher asked her pupils to write a sequel. It was a time when lives were at risk in Beirut because of numerous car bomb attacks. The children wrote a story of total and unconditional forgiveness. The teacher tried to forward the text to Ocelot, thinking that she would never be able to contact him and that, in any case, the director would not be interested. The text reached the filmmaker and deeply moved him, and he decided to again gather his crew of professionals and make a film of the children's story for free. The film is not a classic animation, but more like an animatic, a succession of edited black-and-white drawings designed by Eric Serre and Xavier Riffault, and with backgrounds by Anne-Lise Koelher and Isabelle Ramnou. The original actors took the project to heart and returned to dub voices, and Gabriel Yared again composed the music, all free of charge. The film was called *L'Invité aux Noces* (*The Wedding Guest*) and was completed in 2008. The result of this exciting encounter is a beautiful thirteen-minute short, impressively poetic in its simplicity and sincere innocence.

NOTES

1. "Azur & Asmar. Dossier de presse." Nord-Ouest Films.
2. Ibid.
3. Mouton-Dubosc, Xavier; Berthelon, Thomas. "Michel Ocelot (Kirikou): «Je veux vous faire du bien.»" in *ActuaBd*, October 18, 2012.
4. "Azur & Asmar. Dossier de presse." Nord-Ouest Films.
5. Ibid.
6. Hind O. "«Azur et Asmar est inspiré de l'Algérie …» Entretien avec Michel Ocelot", in *L'Expression*, December 24, 2007.
7. "Azur & Asmar. Dossier de presse." Nord-Ouest Films.
8. "Interview de Michel Ocelot, à l'occasion des 70 ans du Festival de Cannes."
9. *Michel Ocelot. Ma vie d'artiste.* Documentary by Letop Mags, France, 2015.
10. Commin, Jean-Paul; Ganne, Valérie; Brunner, Didier. *Kirikou et Après … 20 Ans de Cinéma d'Animation en France.* Arles: Actes Sud, 2017, p. 53.
11. Terms such as East, Orient, Middle East, Arab world, and so on have been used here because they are so reported in the texts referred to and so named in the interviews cited. However, it is worth noting that these expressions are now dated and have been replaced by more current, non-Eurocentric vocabulary. The more correct term to describe this area is the acronym SWANA (South West Asian and North African), a decolonial word used to distinguish the region in geographical terms, rather than "political terms" as defined by the Western world.
12. Apostolou, Fotini. "Cultural Translations: Transcending Boundaries in Michel Ocelot's Animated Film Azur et Asmar (2006)", in *Communication, Politics & Culture*, University of Thessaloniki, 2009, p. 100.
13. "Azur and Asmar Review", in *Iridium Eye Reviews*, November 7, 2020.
14. White saviorism can be defined as the belief that whites are supposed to rescue, help, teach, and protect their nonwhite counterparts. The term, which is a derivative of White Savior Industrial Complex (WSIC), was coined by Nigerian-American writer Teju Cole in 2012. For further information refer to: Cole, Teju, "The White-Savior Industrial Complex", in *The Atlantic*, March 21, 2012.
15. Apostolou, Fotini. "Cultural Translations: Transcending Boundaries in Michel Ocelot's Animated Film Azur et Asmar (2006)", in

142 ■ Michel Ocelot

Communication, Politics & Culture, University of Thessaloniki, 2009, p. 101.

16. Apostolou, Fotini, *op. cit.*, p. 104.
17. Neupert, Richard. *French Animation History*, p. 138.
18. Apostolou, Fotini, *op. cit.*, p. 105.
19. Apostolou, Fotini, *op. cit.*, p. 100.
20. Mazumdar, Sucheta; Kaiwar, Vasant; Labica, Thierry. *From Orientalism to Postcolonialism. Asia, Europe and the Lineages of Difference.* New York; London: Routledge, 2009, p. 32.
21. "Azur e Asmar. Cartella stampa." Lucky Red.
22. King, C. Richard; Bloodsworth-Lugo, Mary K.; Lugo-Lugo, Carmen R., *op. cit.*, p. 141.
23. Staninger, Christiane. "Disney's Magic Carpet Ride: Aladdin and Women in Islam", in Ayres, Brenda. *The Emperor's Old Groove: Decolonizing Disney's Magic Kingdom.* New York: Peter Lang Publishing, 2003, p. 69.
24. Wise, Christopher. "Notes from the Aladdin Industry: Or, Middle Eastern Folklore in the Era of Multinational Capitalism", in Ayres, Brenda. *The Emperor's Old Groove: Decolonizing Disney's Magic Kingdom.* New York: Peter Lang Publishing, 2003, p. 106.
25. Staninger, Christiane, *op. cit.*, p. 67.
26. Shah, Sabina. *The Portrayal of the Historical Muslim Female on Screen.* Doctoral Thesis, University of Manchester, 2017, p. 121.
27. Zeneise, Gatto. "Esclusiva: intervista a Michel Ocelot", in *afNews.info*, October 1, 2014.
28. Neupert, Richard. *French Animation History*, p. 138.
29. Neupert, Richard. *French Animation History*, p. 135.
30. Shah, Sabina, Neupert, *op. cit.*, p. 122.
31. Neupert, Richard. *French Animation History*, p. 135.
32. Paternò, Cristiana. "Michel Ocelot", in *CinecittàNews*, October 17, 2006.
33. Leffrer, Rebecca. "'Tales of the Night' Director Michel Ocelot Brings Animated 3D to Competition Field (Berlin)", in *The Hollywood Reporter*, February 12, 2011.
34. "Azur & Asmar. Dossier de presse."
35. "An Extensive Personal Interview with Director Michel Ocelot", in *GhibliWorld*, August 29, 2008.
36. Ibid.
37. "Azur e Asmar. Cartella stampa." Lucky Red.

CHAPTER 5

Dilili à Paris, or Beauty Will Save Us

A HOMAGE TO PARIS

Somewhere along the line of his career, Ocelot realised he had staged his films in many locations and various eras, though never once had he chosen the city of Paris as a setting. The idea came to him following a conversation with the renowned Japanese animator Isao Takahata:

> When Director Isao Takahata told me that I could only make Japanese movies in Japan, I realised that I could only make French movies in France. Of course, when I start thinking about a story, I don't really care about country or nationality. I think of myself as a world citizen.[1]

It was then that he began to develop the idea for a film located in the city he lived in and cherished. He was furthermore convinced he would carry out such a project only if he would find a good story. A theme he wanted to address was violence against women and girls. Initially, he reasoned about the possibility of setting a story on an island, a hellish realm where men committed

DOI: 10.1201/9781003292173-6

143

all kinds of prevarications and abuses on women. However, the idea was really too heinous to put into practice and especially knowing he would have to devote himself to the same project for many years. From the union of these two cues, a far more compelling story was conceived: *Dilili à Paris* (*Dilili in Paris* — 2018). The feature was developed over six years and it was produced by the same company that had supported the author in all his works from *Azur & Asmar* onwards: Nord-Ouest Films. Initially, the producer did not agree to take on the new feature; however, he eventually reconsidered and managed to obtain approximately 6.9 million euros to complete the venture, also benefiting from the co-production with Belgium and Germany (Figure 5.1).

Dilili à Paris has as its protagonist a little mixed-race girl, Dilili. Her father was French, her mother came from the indigenous Melanesian Kanak culture. The child Dilili grew up in New Caledonia with an enormous desire for knowledge and discovery of the world. This fervent enthusiasm leads her to secretly embark on a ship bound for France. Dilili, who owes her impeccable French to lessons from the revolutionary and anarchist writer

FIGURE 5.1 *Dilili à Paris*. CGI Animation, 2018. © Nord-Ouest Films / Studio O / Arte France Cinéma / Mars Films / Wild Bunch / Mac Guff Ligne / Artemis Productions / Senator Film Produktion.

Louise Michel, politely introduces herself to every new person she meets. Louise Michel was Dilili's governess while forced to stay in New Caledonia following her deportation from France. In Paris, the little girl befriends Orel, a gentle and charming young man who, on his tricycle, accompanies her as she explores the city. Together, they try to solve the mystery of the Master Males, a criminal sect that is kidnapping girls in Paris with the aim of controlling them and bringing them, literally, to their knees. Orel, who is a delivery boy and has therefore come to know and be loved by the city that matters, brings Dilili into contact with a host of well-known personalities of the time, all of whom are eager to help in her investigations. With the support of Orel and the opera singer Emma Calvé, the girl manages to unearth the sect's lair, hidden in the sewers, and, after many vicissitudes, free the imprisoned girls, taking them back to their families (Figure 5.2).

The feature film depicts a fascinating and colourful journey, immersing viewers in the discovery of the French capital during

FIGURE 5.2 Dilili and Orel. *Dilili à Paris*. CGI Animation, 2018. © Nord-Ouest Films / Studio O / Arte France Cinéma / Mars Films / Wild Bunch / Mac Guff Ligne / Artemis Productions / Senator Film Produktion.

the Belle Époque and its enthralling cultural life. Setting the movie in one of Paris' most enchanting times had multiple motivations for Ocelot. Initially, the choice was made mainly for aesthetic reasons: It would allow him to reproduce elaborate Art Nouveau architecture and elegant costumes, and enable viewers to enjoy the splendour of art at the turn of the nineteenth century into the twentieth. Furthermore, he said, "it is a period far enough back for us to dream and imagine, but also close enough that we can easily find documentation".[2] It was easier to retain a fairy-tale atmosphere, as the long women's dresses of the epoch allowed for dreams and fantasies of fairies and princesses. As he conducted research and gathered documentation, he also discovered a city populated by numerous outstanding personalities, active in every field of knowledge, from art to science, and technology to the world of entertainment. He tried to pay tribute to each of these, bringing many of them together with the protagonist and her companion.

In the company of Dilili and Orel, viewers find themselves enjoying animated can-can shows by colourful dancers at the Moulin Rouge, and the liveliness of Parisian nightclubs. In one of these, we meet Henri de Toulouse-Lautrec, a great artist, and genius of advertising graphics at the turn of the century, along with many of the real figures depicted in his posters – such as cabaret artist Aristide Bruant, as depicted in one of his 1897 lithographs. Toulouse-Lautrec, greatly admired by Ocelot, is among the characters who longest accompany the protagonist on her discovery of the mysteries of Paris. The list of celebrities is endless. Among the ranks of the art world, we meet painters such as Suzanne Valadon, Claude Monet, Henri Matisse, and Le Douanier Rousseau; great sculptors such as Camille Claudel, Auguste Rodin, and Constantin Brâncuși; composers Claude Debussy and Erik Satie; Marcel Proust, at the time he was still an aspiring writer. Ocelot also wanted to pay homage to the world of science by introducing us to the chemist Louis Pasteur and the great Polish scientist Marie Curie, as well as many other illustrious women of the past. In the film appear the actress Sarah Bernhardt; the art collector Gertrude Stein; the poet and socialist feminist Anna de Noailles; the writer and theatre actress Colette. Among these exceptional women, a prominent place was reserved for the soprano Emma Calvé, who replaced the initial candidate for the role, Sarah Bernhardt. Calvé was chosen because she was equally well-known and loved at the time, but forgotten nowadays. Calvé plays the part of a sort of fairy who intervenes whenever help is needed. She was played by French opera singer Natalie Dessay, who, in addition to showcasing her remarkable singing skills, also lent her voice to the speaking part, giving an admirable performance.

Ocelot had chosen many more characters but soon realised the limitations of representing Belle Époque Paris: "There were only white people. This had never happened to me in previous films! I felt it was an impoverishment for my audience and for myself".[3] He was able to find in some prints by Toulouse-Lautrec a Chinese bartender, probably originally from San Francisco, and a clown of Cuban descent, Chocolat – the pseudonym of Raphael Padilla, a circus star in Paris around 1900. In a painting by Jaques-Émile Blanche, he noticed a Tunisian poet and, in some period photographs, a Maharajah fascinated by France. Reading the diary of Louise Michel, deported to New Caledonia, he discovered that she had taken a great interest in the country, its customs, legends, and above all her work as a governess for young Kanak children. Based on those findings, the director imagined Dilili, a sprightly and bright little girl who combined two very distant cultures.

The film admirably reconstructs the Paris of the time, conveys the atmosphere, and effectively succeeds in captivating and astounding the audience. Convinced he could not reproduce the capital more beautifully than it is in reality, Ocelot chose to use photographic images of Parisian monuments and views, then retouched them on the computer (Figure 5.3).

FIGURE 5.3 Dilili, Orel and Toulouse-Lautrec on the tricycle. In the background, Place Vendôme. *Dilili à Paris.* CGI Animation, 2018. © Nord-Ouest Films / Studio O / Arte France Cinéma / Mars Films / Wild Bunch / Mac Guff Ligne / Artemis Productions / Senator Film Produktion.

The filmmaker took around fifteen thousand photos over a period of four years while walking around the city or whizzing through the streets on his roller skates. He would wake up at the first light of dawn to get a view of the city in daylight but almost empty, so as to limit the number of elements to be removed from the photos. "The changes were minimal because I wanted to show reality. Of course, we removed all contemporary marks, street signs, cars, motorbikes, rubbish cans. Sometimes we removed cigarette butts and litter, but this is Paris as it appears today",[4] he said.

Historical context furthermore turned into an opportunity to celebrate French history and its cultural richness. Ocelot had already addressed his country's past, even if not explicitly, providing it with an extraordinary interpretation, as already highlighted in the first chapter. Here too, he masterfully recreated the flavour of an era. Toulouse-Lautrec, and more generally the graphic art of those years, are an important visual reference point for Ocelot, orientating his stylistic choices in the representation of human figures. Many of the characters and extras in the film are indeed depicted by referring directly to some of their

FIGURE 5.4   The celebrities of the Irish American Bar. *Dilili à Paris*. CGI Animation, 2018. © Nord-Ouest Films / Studio O / Arte France Cinéma / Mars Films / Wild Bunch / Mac Guff Ligne / Artemis Productions / Senator Film Produktion.

works. Among them is a famous lady in a black hat and dress, taken from an 1893 print, *Divan Japonaise*, an advertisement for the eponymous nightclub (Figure 5.4).

The woman is the can-can dancer Jane Avril, who has become an icon of the Belle Époque, precisely owing to the numerous artworks dedicated to her by her friend Toulouse-Lautrec. The artist's prints are also shown hanging along the streets and in the interiors of Parisian buildings, along with others, such as the poster advertising the Lumière brothers' cinema, designed by Marcellin Auzolle in 1896 and one of Alphonse Mucha's innumerable lithographs depicting Sarah Bernhardt.

To define the aesthetic of the characters, the approach adopted for *Azur & Asmar* was used as a reference. Faces in 3D showed discrete modelling with frontal lighting, the clothing was instead flat, avoiding shadows, sculptural quality, and chiaroscuro. Again, Ocelot preferred an artificial and stylised look, tending towards flatness, as he had already experienced in all his other productions. The choice was determined by matters of taste; it was also the most practical and least expensive option. Budgetary restraints required supplementing the 3D animation by using the cheaper 2D in parallel. He stated:

> 2D has to be drawn with hand strokes and we made a similar choice for 3D animation. This imitation of the stroke, from real 3D, is very sophisticated. We improved

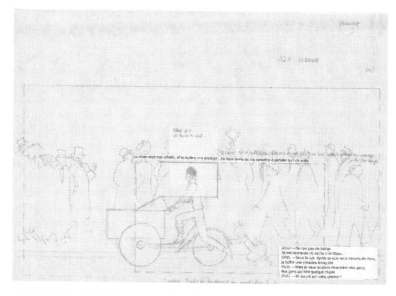

FIGURE 5.5 Dilili helps Orel push the tricycle. Scene layout. *Dilili à Paris*, 2018. © Ocelot-Studio O.

on what the Mac Guff studio had perfected for *Kirikou et les Hommes et les Femmes,* and this is the direction I like. I find that realistic 3D does not allow one to dream fully".[5] (Figures 5.5 and 5.6)

The figures were then integrated into the backgrounds consisting of lightly retouched photographs of important sights and monuments. Many Parisian spots are traversed in the course of this modern fable: Place de la Concorde and Place Vendôme; the Jardin des Tuileries; the Marché aux fleurs Madeleine; the Théâtre de l'Atelier; the Petit and Grand Palais; Montmartre district; and Castel Béranger, where Dilili is housed, a building considered a true manifesto of Art Nouveau.

While the project was struggling to find funding, the city of Paris opened its doors to the director:

FIGURE 5.6 Dilili helps Orel push the tricycle. 2D and 3D animation on photograph. *Dilili à Paris*. CGI Animation, 2018. © Nord-Ouest Films / Studio O / Arte France Cinéma / Mars Films / Wild Bunch / Mac Guff Ligne / Artemis Productions / Senator Film Produktion.

I was able to photograph the Art Nouveau of the Bouillon Racine, a very modest restaurant at the time, which retained its original décor from 1900. I was also able to photograph Maxim's restaurant, also from 1900, but of a different style and not modest. This is what you see on the first floor of the Eiffel Tower in my film. I also benefited from real access to the sewers of Paris, where friendly sewage workers went out of their way to help me in my research. [...] And, by a miracle, I had privileged access to the Musée d'Orsay, [...] to the Musée Rodin, to the Musée du Quai Branly, to the Musée Marmottan Monet, to the Paris Opera, from the basement to the roof!".[6]

Much of the action takes place at the Opéra Garnier, where Dilili and Orel meet with Emma Calvé. The interior displays monumental staircases, red velvets, gilded stucco, frescoed ceilings, crystal chandeliers, and a myriad of mirrors. Ocelot also exploited the curiosity of Parisians to set part of the story in the

Opéra's most mysterious and inaccessible place. The lake that can be seen in the film is, in fact, a real existing water basin underneath the building, pre-existing its construction and incorporated into the foundations with a watertight system due to the impossibility of moving the construction elsewhere. Calvé crosses this underground lake using a swan-shaped boat, which the director designed inspired by the craft that Louis II of Bavaria had ordered, built in an artificial cave under his castle in Linderhof, Germany. Starting from these cues, the filmmaker immerses us in a fairy-tale scenario, the fruit of his fervent imagination and refined taste.

The interior of Sarah Bernhardt's apartment has not been preserved until the present day, so it was thoroughly reconstructed and furnished with highly sought-after furniture. Among them, the *Aube et Crépuscule* bed designed by Émile Gallé in 1904, made of ebony, mother-of-pearl, and iridescent glass. Regarding Berhardt's cheetah – it really existed. With the money she had earned from her theatrical success in London, Sarah Berhardt went to Liverpool Zoo to purchase some exotic animals, including a very young cheetah. The garden in which the animal roams, with Dilili on its back, takes inspiration from the paintings of Henri Rousseau, already used as a visual source for forest settings in the features starring Kirikou.

Unlike in past works, there is a very different regard for camera movements, more studied and articulated, more inherently cinematic. It is not unlikely the filmmaker may have made this choice to reinforce the relationship which, precisely in those years, was being created between live-action cinema, in its first steps, and the French capital, a major centre of elaboration for this new language. Especially in the staging of the flashback narration, the employment of the black frame strongly recalls the effects frequently utilised in early cinema. Similarly, the narration relates to coeval culture, taking as a reference the literary model of the *roman-feuilleton*, or serial. The serial was a genre of novel, very popular from the early decades of the nineteenth century onwards and published in newspapers or magazines in episodes of a few pages, and aimed at a mass readership. The central narrative plot that Dilili has to unravel is precisely a detective story, common in these kinds of novels. This prompt is mingled with various influences and languages, including architecture, photography, cinema, interior design, and painting.

For the original soundtrack, the successful collaboration with Gabriel Yared was renewed. Yared, who really appreciated the story, was involved from the beginning, allowing him time to ponder over his compositions. After the script and some drawings, he was given the animatic – the entire movie assembled through sketches, with dialogue, prepared before any production. Together, he and Ocelot decided what music was essential to record before animation, in particular, the piece *Le Soleil et la Pluie* (*The Sun and the Rain*), which recurs throughout the film in different forms. Once the animation was finished, they worked together to determine which moments should be supported by the music. In this case, too, Yared's music added considerable value to the atmosphere of the entire movie. The original score blends perfectly with pieces chose from period repertoire, such as *Gnossienne no. 1* played on the piano directly by Satie, while Orel and Chocolat dance. Yared's melodies and moods seem to come straight from turn-of-the-century France, and the song *Le Soleil et la Pluie*, composed by Yared with lyrics by Ocelot, will be pleasantly stuck in your mind for a long time (Figure 5.7).

It can be said that the overall accuracy and consistency of this movie is even more outstanding than in previous works, probably also because of the greater number of documentation sources available. The tension between intentions bordering on documentary research and aesthetic refinement led Ocelot to combine very different images: Realistic backdrops along with the total artificiality of human figures. This whole exhibition of magnificence, which almost seems to clash with the dark theme of the story, has an intrinsic value in Ocelot' poetics, as already mentioned in the first chapter. With *Dilili à Paris*, the

FIGURE 5.7   2D character's design. The figures are designed as artic-
ulated puppets. *Dilili à Paris*. CGI Animation, 2018. © Nord-Ouest
Films / Studio O / Arte France Cinéma / Mars Films / Wild Bunch /
Mac Guff Ligne / Artemis Productions / Senator Film Produktion.

conception for which the display of beauty is itself a political act
is brought to full fruition. Romanian-French playwright Eugène
Ionesco wrote:

> Modern man, the universal man, is the busy man, who
> has no time, who is a prisoner of necessity. [...] If one
> does not understand the usefulness of the useless, the
> uselessness of the useful, one does not understand art;
> and a country where one does not understand art is a
> country of slaves or robots, a country of unhappy people,
> of people who do not laugh or smile, a country without
> spirit; where there is no humour, no laughter, there is
> anger and hatred".[7]

Likewise, the pursuit of flawlessness is for Ocelot a statement
in itself, a method of delivering a message: What enriches a
society can change its mentality, push it to understanding and
openness. A form of the utility of beauty, as opposed to the
utilitarianism of commercial products. In the director's intentions, this notion combines with the film's humanist message,

FIGURE 5.8   Dilili, Orel, and Emma Calvé on the swan-shaped boat. *Dilili à Paris*. CGI Animation, 2018. © Nord-Ouest Films / Studio O / Arte France Cinéma / Mars Films / Wild Bunch / Mac Guff Ligne / Artemis Productions / Senator Film Produktion.

which calls for understanding, rejection of injustice, and the breaking of established norms:

> What has always been the intention with my work is to add beauty to the beauty of the world, and alongside beauty for the eyes I seek moral beauty. And this moral beauty I seek by always being sincere and honest with my films. I never cheat. I hope with my stories to grant people dignity"[8] (Figure 5.8).

A HUMANIST MESSAGE

Dilili à Paris was released in October 2018, preceded by a premiere at the Annecy Film Festival. The film was very successful at festivals, winning several awards including the prestigious César Award for Best Animated film, a major prize in France. However, audience comments on social media and critics' reviews were roughly split into two main factions: Many celebrated the film for the beauty of its settings and the boldness of its themes, whereas others criticised it harshly. Some reviews judged negatively the general aesthetic and in particular the animation,[9] which they considered clunky and unnatural. Other criticisms focused on the somewhat disjointed script,[10] along with the failure to find a harmonious solution that could mediate between its two target audiences, children and adults.[11] Considered overly preachy, concerned with educational intent aimed at children, and too long-winded to be enjoyed with delight by adults,[12] the more shocking scenes would make it unapproachable for a younger audience. Yet, many children interviewed in cinemas commented on the film in enthusiastic tones, and the director reported how during the screenings child audiences applauded at the moment of the girls' release, which moved him strongly.[13]

Nonetheless, if the remarks regarding animation are somewhat specious, the criticism concerning the content is based on much more valid grounds. Admittedly, it can be argued that the scene showing the girls on all fours and covered in black drapes is shocking even to an adult viewer. The tone of the narration quickly shifts from a cultured fantasy to a dystopian[14] atmosphere reminiscent of Margaret Atwood's works. This horrifying vision, a metaphor that plastically describes the oppressive condition of women around the world, leaves a sense of disturbance in viewers, and therefore the choice not to sugarcoat a topic as harsh as gender violence might be appreciated. However, the most questionable core lies in the ambiguities that a substantial part of the public perceived in this specific passage. Repeatedly, it emerged how much this view was considered insulting to people of Islamic background.[15] The young girls are covered from head to toe in long black cloaks, considered by many to closely resemble a chador or a niqāb, which has been identified as a statement against the Islamic veil. In the wake of the first comments, Ocelot quickly replied, publicly denying any intention of making specific reference. Black had been chosen as a symbol of death, rejection, and violence.[16] It can be argued the imagery was most likely inspired by the aesthetics of nineteenth-century Masonic lodges. In spite of that, the coincidence with current stereotypes of Islamic women was often remarked upon in reviews of the film.[17] Hence, although there was no intentionality in delivering this message, as I believe, Ocelot's inattention, even if involuntary, was in not realising that this sequence might offend many people.[18]

Such inconveniences, moreover, become harder to justify when combined with other criticalities emerging more clearly in the course of the film, and substantiated by the author's own words. The French capital is shown in all the grandeur of the Belle Époque, a period indeed exceptional for artistic and scientific ferment in France. For Ocelot, the homage to the history and culture of his country also passed through the accurate representation of the architecture and introduction to personalities that contributed to making that vibrant historical moment great. The in-depth research to restore the complexity of Parisian society of the time allowed him to stage racialised characters such as Chocolat, the renowned clown. Nonetheless, this operation doesn't exclusively aim to bring to light a forgotten historical truth, namely the presence of Black people in France at the time and their active role in the development of modern art.[19] The press stressed how, ultimately, Ocelot's purpose seems to be the promotion of French civilisation, the openness of its society, greatness, and civilising mission.[20]

There would be nothing wrong with enthusiastically recounting one's country's history and culture, yet it becomes an uncritical glorification insofar as racist issues are trivialised and colonial responsibilities are erased. The opening scene of the film shows a depiction of a human zoo, a horrendous colonial invention, displayed with total indifference. It is not described as abnormal and inhuman; and since the human zoo is no longer mentioned in the rest of the film and neither Dilili nor the adults around her seem to be bothered by it, this amounts to trivialising a scene that should horrify us.[21] It could be argued that malice is in the eye of the beholder, yet, to dispel any doubt, Ocelot himself stated that these villages "allowed Western artists to progress, whether in the plastic arts, dance or music. There were horrors, but not everything is bad".[22] This totally Eurocentric view of the horrors produced by colonialism runs throughout the feature film. On another occasion,[23] the filmmaker reported his surprise over the prosperity of French society and the flourishing of its cultural life as the country was recovering after a bitter defeat at the hands of the Prussians. What the director seems to ignore is how France's fortunes were largely due to the colonial empire it controlled and from which it extracted goods and profits. In *Dilili à Paris,* Ocelot's alleged intent was to emphasise the senselessness of racism and try to highlight the path to tolerance through the transformation of Lebeuf's character. The man, in the course of the story, moves from his initial hostility towards Dilili, whom he discriminates against, to an understanding of his error. From being an antagonist he becomes part of the ranks of the positive figures and helps the child to free the other little girls. The educational intent is noble; however, it betrays a view common to many Europeans, including thinkers on the radical left, as the anthropologist Miguel Mellino pointed out in his writings.[24] In fact, Mellino argued that much of the European progressive left is inclined to view racism as external to the development of the modern Western capitalist economy, a mere deviation, the result of ignorance and an exclusively individual matter. However, to fully understand the phenomenon of racism, its structural nature must be evidenced. The experience of colonialism, moreover, cannot be regarded as a premodern regurgitation, but a real laboratory of modernity. As is recurrent among a large population of Europeans who have forgotten their colonial past, Ocelot provides us with a faultless rendition of contemporary French society. The close interdependence between European prosperity and colonial atrocities, which allows for a thorough investigation of the mechanisms of colonialism and contemporary racism, is not considered in *Dilili à Paris*. It is not possible to be fully anti-racist without criticising the system that has generated and nurtured racism. Therefore, the film creates some short circuits that break the enchantment of the narrative and the effectiveness of the message of openness and dialogue.

In light of these observations, it is also excessive to define *Dilili à Paris* as "a feminist fable", as has very often been the case.[25] Firstly, it is the director himself who clarifies this point, stressing that he does not consider himself a feminist and specifying, rather, how the movie carries a humanist message.[26] Ocelot is right to define his work as such, as the message conveyed is clearly imbued with a universalist culture that promulgates equality without taking specificities into account, minimising the role of specific oppressions and privileges. The feminist perspective on women's issues has been enriched and complicated in recent years precisely due to the increased participation of members of marginalised and oppressed groups in debates on this matter, intersecting with other theories and claims, including anti-racist struggles and decolonial thought.[27] In relation to these new upheavals in the international intellectual panorama, considering the film a vehicle for feminist values is the result of superficial evaluation.

All these critical elements significantly detract from the film's educational message, especially since the protagonist is a delightful and charming figure. Dilili, like Kirikou before her, is a catalyst heroine who takes on the injustices she sees in society and goes in search of the means to solve them. She is a complex character, appreciable for her agency and determination. Her curiosity and great courage make her an ideal reference point for many little girls, who can identify with her. Praised as a "multi-racial pretty brown girl who [...] is well aware of the effect that her appearance has on others",[28] this aspect does not define her and keeps her away from the trope of the racialised tragic character. She was also described as a heroine who embodied the very essence of pluck and resilience.[29] Choosing a young girl also had the enormous advantage of completely excluding romance from the feature's storyline. Dilili is interested in everything she perceives around her and during the course of the film we see her engaged in figuring out what she likes best, showing an aptitude for many different activities and considering as many professions for her future. Romantic love is never mentioned; on the contrary, a strong emphasis is placed on extra-familiar relationships. A particularly poignant message is the statement about how we are all people in need of affection and love; it is touching to see the little girl learning the art of cuddling from Emma Calvé. As an orphan, Dilili longs for hugs and tenderness and in the course of the story receives much tenderness and consideration.[30] Due to her resourcefulness and power, Dilili was elected in 2018 as UNICEF's messenger for the empowerment of girls and their right to education.

A FORAY INTO LIVE-ACTION CINEMA: *PABLO-PARIS-SATIE*

With *Dilili à Paris,* Ocelot wanted to celebrate an "intense civilisation",[31] and to show the different forms it took. Among the many aspects considered was dance, and he entrusted the circus performer Chocolat with the task of illustrating this art masterfully. The filmmaker wanted the animators to carefully animate the dancer's movements, so he decided to go to the Opéra to enlist the help of a professional. The dancer Pablo Legasa, Premier dancer of the Paris Opera Ballet, danced with dedication and creativity the piece chosen to accompany the scene, Erik Satie's *Gnossienne no. 1.*

Fascinated by the result and moved by Legasa's generosity, the director decided to turn a poor-quality video into a live-action film that would do justice to the poetry of this dance. "*I told myself that we had to record his magnificent work again, this time in conditions worthy of his art*",[32] he stated. Ocelot had never directed a live-action film before, and, with *Pablo-Paris-Satie,* he confirmed the vocation for poetic simplicity already shown in his many works. Legasa dances on a Parisian rooftop with the backdrop of the city illuminated by an enveloping and delicate light, following the director's few instructions to "breathe the music",[33] and not to exaggerate in virtuosity. The short was released in 2020, directed by Michel Ocelot, and was produced by the Paris Opera's digital Stage, 3eScène, a company that aims to promote the heritage of Opéra.

NOTES

1. "Interview with Michel Ocelot of Dilili and Paris Time Trip, which Captures Beautiful Paris in a Realistic Movie", in *Gigazine*, August 12, 2019.
2. "Dilili à Paris. Cartella stampa." Nord-Ouest Films.
3. "Dilili à Paris. Dossier de presse." Nord-Ouest Films.
4. Personal communication with Michel Ocelot, February 14, 2023.
5. "Dilili à Paris. Dossier de presse." Nord-Ouest Films.
6. Ibid.
7. Ionesco Eugène. *Note e contronote: Scritti sul teatro.* Torino: Einaudi, 1965, pp. 142–143.
8. Ugolini, Chiara. "'Dilili a Parigi'. Michel Ocelot: 'Un cartoon femminista? Umanista, direi'", in *La Repubblica*, April 29, 2019.
9. Debruge, Peter. "Film Review: 'Dilili in Paris'", in *Variety*, October 4, 2019.
10. Dobroiu, Ştefan. "Review: Dilili in Paris", in *Cineuropa*, October 16, 2019.
11. Guedj, Philippe. "Dilili à Paris divise le Festival d'Annecy", in *Le Point Pop*, June 12, 2018.
12. Lorfèvre, Alain. "'Dilili à Paris'. Un conte maladroit un brin moralisateur", in *La Libre*, October 24, 2018.
13. Ezzakhrajy, Myriam. "Michel Ocelot. Un féministe engagé", in *Femmes du Maroc*, April 26, 2019.
14. It should be pointed out that the more appropriate term here would be uchronia, as it is the replacement of events that really happened in a particular historical period with others that are fictional, but verisimilar. Dystopia describes or represents, instead, a future state of affairs.
15. Fatima Ouassak, Fatima. Michel Ocelot / 2018. Dilili à Paris, Le Genre & L'écran, November 20, 2018.
16. Ezzakhrajy, Myriam, *op. cit.*
17. Guedj, Philippe, *op. cit.*
18. Lorfèvre, Alain, *op. cit.*

19. The active presence and centrality of certain racialised characters in late nineteenth-century society was the subject of study to coincide with the exhibition Posing Modernity: The Black Model From Manet and Matisse to Today, organised by Columbia University's Wallach Art Gallery in collaboration with the Musée d'Orsay. Curator and art historian Denise Murrell pointed out, for instance, how the model Laure, the black woman painted in Manet's painting Olympia, was a person portrayed by the painter on several occasions and was considered by him to be no different from the others in his entourage. For further information refer to: *Le modèle noir: de Gericault a Matisse*. Paris: Musee d'Orsay/Flammarion, 2019.

20. Cailleau, Emma, Moreau, Gérard, Barrault, Michèle. "'Dilili à Paris' ou l'escamotage de la colonisation" in *Billets d'Afrique*, January 26, 2019.

21. Ibid.

22. Ibid.

23. "Dilili à Paris. Dossier de presse." Nord-Ouest Films.

24. Mellino, Miguel. *La Critica Postcoloniale: Decolonizzazione, Capitalismo e Cosmopolitismo nei Postcolonial Studies*. Milano: Meltemi, 2021.

25. Provencher, Normand. "'Dilili à Paris', la fable féministe de Michel Ocelot", in *Le Soleil*, December 6, 2018.

26. Ugolini, Chiara. "'Dilili a Parigi', Michel Ocelot: 'Un cartoon femminista? Umanista, direi'", in *La Repubblica*, April 29, 2019.

27. The term intersectional feminism was coined by Kimberlé Crenshaw, an American law professor, in 1989. Intersectional feminism got an approach that on the experience of those who are object of concurrent and overlapping forms of oppression in order to understand the depth of inequalities and the relationships between them. For further information refer to: Crenshaw, Kimberlé "Mapping the Margins: Intersectionality, Identity Politics, and Violence against Women of Color", in *Stanford Law Review* Vol. 43, No. 6 (Jul., 1991), pp. 1241–1299.

28. Nicholas, Lynnette. "#NYICFF19 Review: 'Dilili in Paris'", in *BlackGirlNerd*.

29. Fagerholm Matt, "Reviews: Dilili in Paris", in *Roger Erbert.com*, October 04, 2019.

30. Ibid.

31. "Inteview with Michel Ocelot. Interview conducted by Marie d'Harcourt," Opéra National de Paris, 2020.
32. Michel Ocelot's official website.
33. "Inteview with Michel Ocelot. Interview conducted by Marie d'Harcourt," Opéra National de Paris, 2020.

Appendix 1

I n October 2022, Ocelot's latest film *Le Pharaon, le Sauvage et la Princesse* (*The Pharaoh, the Savage and the Princess*) was released. It is a feature composed of three separate stories, all very different in taste and atmosphere. Each of the fables is introduced by a woman in work clothes who plays the narrator, to a crowd of people whom we only see in black silhouette, in the middle of a construction site. The director drew this setting in the very first days of the lockdown due to the pandemic, the scenario thus assuming the role of a positive exhortation not to lose heart and to resume activities when possible. The first tale is set in ancient Egypt, which allowed the filmmaker to pay homage to a visual universe he had always admired and which served as a source of inspiration on many occasions. The second story is recounted with the elegance of black silhouettes, which perfectly suited the medieval setting. The scenery takes its cue from the grandiose landscapes and architecture of the Auvergne, a verdant region of central France. The third is a tale of love and gastronomy, set in Ottoman Turkey. A feast for the eyes, accompanied by the sensuality of the culinary delights depicted in a charming and opulent style. The feature title was initially supposed to be *Le Pharaon, le Sauvage et la Maîtresse des Confitures* (*The Pharaoh, the Savage, and the Jam Lady*). It was eventually changed for commercial reasons and because it was too long.

The director then found a clever way to take a step back from his own traditions by inserting the line "We are fed up with princesses!" in the opening dialogues. The first short was developed at McGuff Belgium animation studio, while the other two were by a team located in the EJT-Laboratory studio at Saint Quirin in Lorraine, plus some professionals working remotely. The crew that moved to the forest of Lorraine had the largest slice of work, a very young and enthusiastic group. Ocelot also settled in Saint Quirin to supervise the work. It took three and a half years to complete the movie, not including the writing of the scripts – and two years, with great difficulty, to find the necessary funding. The production is by Nord-Ouest Films.

INTERVIEW WITH MICHEL OCELOT

February 14, 2023

How did the film project Le Pharaon, le Sauvage et la Princesse *come about? Why did you choose these three stories?*

It took me six years to shoot *Dilili in Paris* – like my previous features. When the animators, having finished their work, left, suddenly my brain was allowed to think of something else, something else meaning another film. After this film, which was heavy in many ways, I wanted to move on to much lighter things, after an opera, to return to the ditty – which can live longer than an opera.

I had already noticed years ago a tale collected by Henri Pourrat, *Le Conte du Beau Sauvage.* I kept more of the original beautiful tale than I usually do. Then I leafed through another collection of stories from Morocco. In one tale, which was about something else entirely, I noted a young girl's declared interest in a handsome doughnut merchant, a reminder of stories from *The Arabian Nights.* This made me want to do a whimsical "Turquerie", like Molière or Mozart, a "comedy-ballet" in exotic costumes without aiming at historical truth. I set it in Istanbul to take advantage of the extraordinary costumes and scenery, but the prince, the princess, and the ladies-in-waiting are more like the Trianon than the Topkapi. I did take into account the nations that crossed paths in this extraordinary region, Anatolia, with the shouts of the merchants in the market.

The first tale is one of those surprises of life. The President-Director of the Louvre invited me to come and see him, to consider a collaboration. It was with great pleasure that I met Jean-Luc Martinez. I began by telling him that I had no idea what I could do with the Louvre. In the course of our conversation, he told me about a major exhibition in preparation called *Pharaon des Deux Terres, l'épopée africaine des rois de Napata*. This caused a great chemical reaction in my brain. On the one hand, there was the Egyptian civilisation which has fascinated me since my first year at school, on the other hand, there was Black Africa which is part of my childhood – reinforced by the story of *Kirikou et la Sorciére*. I then proposed to make an animated film on the subject and asked for all the documents from the exhibition. I was able to see the preparation of such an exhibition. I read the translation of the Dream Stele. It's about a Kushite king – North Sudan – who dreams that he conquers Egypt. When he wakes up, he does so and succeeds. I followed this journey quite closely in my script and amplified a nice element of this dynasty: The Kushites were not cruel and knew how to forgive. The story had the approval of the authorities at the Louvre, which participated in the production of the film (Figure 6.1).

Can you tell us something about your experience of working with the Louvre?

I first conceived things on my own, with knowledge and a taste for Egypt, which allowed me to make quite accurate images. But let's go back to my past. I was continually reproached for the representation of women's breasts, from *Kirikou* to *Dilili*, to *Azur & Asmar*, about which some American journalists asked me if I would agree to cut the opening scene in order to be

FIGURE 6.1 *Le Pharaon*. *Le Pharaon, le Sauvage et la Princesse*. CGI Animation, 2022. © Nord-Ouest Films / Studio O / Les Productions du Ch'timi / Musée du Louvre / Artémis Productions.

distributed in the United States. That scene simply showed a nursemaid breastfeeding a small child … For this new film, I instinctively hid the breasts of the princesses and goddesses. I am appalled by this today. Fortunately, Vincent Rondot shouted "But you can't do that! Everyone was bare-chested in Egypt!" (laughing). I happily replaced the dresses at the right height, under the chest, and draped the regent diagonally, following the Kushite fashion, showing her generous left breast. Everything else was checked by Vincent Rondot and his team, and it was a great pleasure.

How many people worked on the film? What type of work organisation characterised *Le Pharaon, le Sauvage et la Princesse*?

About forty people. There was no particular organisation. There were two animation teams, one in Brussels with ten people for the story about the pharaoh, the other in Saint-Quirin, a village in Lorraine, with about twenty people, for the other two films. These small numbers allowed us to work in a friendly manner where everyone understood each other.

What role did the musicians play in the production of this film?

I asked Pascal Le Pennec to compose the music. I involved the composer from the beginning of the project, as usual. We judged together, by viewing the animatic, the moments where we should have music. There were two phases in the making of music: The music where we sing and dance, which is made before the animation, and the accompanying music, which is made after the animation. First, there was an extremely precise model, then the recording with the Orchestre Symphonique de Bretagne [now called the Orchestre National de Bretagne].

On which visual sources did you mainly draw inspiration for each of the stories?

For *Le Pharaon*, a lifetime of love for this art, twenty-five books in my library on this civilisation, and the re-readings of Vincent Rondot, who heads the Egyptian department of the Louvre and who is the specialist of the Kushite dynasty. For *Le Sauvage*, the indispensable Violet Le Duc for the medieval architecture and furniture, my own photos of Auvergne for the nature and some buildings. For *La Princesse*, very precisely I have taken all the costumes from *Costume de la Turquie. Soixante gravures de Octavien Dalvimart* (*The Costume of Turkey. Illustrated by a Series of Engravings by Octavien Dalvimart*), an English publication of 1802. The palace owes a lot to the Topkapı Palace in Istanbul and some splendid nineteenth-century follies. And, all the time, wanderings on the Internet (Figure 6.2).

What messages did you want to communicate with this work?

The message and the immediate pleasure of a screening go hand in hand. I think about the Moral and I also care about the Beautiful Show. The first tale encourages boldness, action, resistance to bad advice, and non-violence. The second is about violence and victorious resistance to that violence, accompanied by forgiveness. The last one is again about resistance to bad laws

FIGURE 6.2 *La Princesse. Le Pharaon, le Sauvage et la Princesse.* CGI Animation, 2022. © Nord-Ouest Films / Studio O / Les Productions du Ch'timi / Musée du Louvre / Artémis Productions.

or orders, about liberation that leads to a life of one's own choosing.

What project are you currently working on?
I am working on three projects. A rather orthodox feature film set in the present day, a medium-length film based on an Italian fairy tale set in fifteenth-century Tuscany, and, further on, a large "Europe through fairy tale" project, a series.

THIERRY BURON, HEAD OF SET DESIGN, TELLS US ABOUT HIS EXPERIENCE WORKING ON *LE PHARAON, LE SAUVAGE ET LA PRINCESSE*

13 March 2023

I started in animation by the greatest of coincidences. An advertisement from an animation studio in Blois, pinned on the walls of a job centre in Toulouse. When I started to work with Michel Ocelot I was developing a project for a television series that never saw the light of day. Then I worked with Michel in the making of *Le Pharaon, le Sauvage et la Princesse,* holding the position of head set designer. So, I arrived on a Monday morning with a cup of coffee and biscuits, and for a week my work consisted of leafing through piles of books. Most of them had bookmarks corresponding to the storyboard boxes. Countries treated in the film, great painters, Violet le Duc, etc ... The documentation was varied but central. Michel likes to say "If a carpenter watches my film, I want him to be able to marvel at the wooden doors, furniture, or windows!". The sources of inspiration are above all given by Michel, who knows exactly what he wants. I think Michel Ocelot is an artist whose medium is film. We were not in an animation studio, we were in an artist's studio! We knew that we were going to participate in the creation of an artwork. It is so simple to say, but also scary. Everyone's generosity did the rest. Speaking of generosity, I think of Eminé, Ethienne, and Luigi from EJT-Labo in St Quirin. The work consisted of scrupulously following Michel's instructions. We were like Benedictines designing beautiful bindings. Saint-Quirin, lost in the middle of the woods, lent itself perfectly to this experience.

Appendix 2

FILMS

1972
Gril-Minute (SEB)
Animated short advertisement movie
Production: Trinacra Films

La Drogue
Animated information short film
Mixed techniques
Production: Trinacra Films

1973
Le Tabac
Animated information short film
Mixed techniques
Production: Trinacra Films

1976
Gédéon
Animated TV series, 60 episodes of 5 minutes each
Cut-out animation
Production: Trinacra Films

1979
Les 3 Inventeurs
13-minute animated short film
Cut-out animation
Production: aaa production

AWARDS
BAFTA (British Academy of Film and Television Award) for the
Best Animated Film, London (UK),1981.
César Award nomination for the Best Animated Short Film,
Paris (France), 1981.
First Prize, Animafest, Zagreb (Croatia), 1980.
Golden Trophy, International Film Festival, Odense (Denmark),
1980

1981
Les Filles de l'égalité
1-minute animated short film
Traditional animation
Production: aaa production

Beyond Oil
2-minute corporate movie
Mixed techniques
Production: aaa production

1982
La Légende du Pauvre Bossu
7-minute animated short film
Mixed techniques

AWARDS
César Award for the Best Animated Short Film, Paris (France),
1983
Best of Annecy tour, USA and Canada

1984
La Princesse Insensible
Animated TV series, 13 episodes of 4 minutes each
Mixed techniques
Production: aaa production

AWARDS
Audience Prize, Odense International Short Film Festival,
Odense (Denmark), 1985
Short Film Jury Prize, International Festival, Bourg-en-Bresse
(France), 1984

1987
Les 4 Vœux
5-minute animated short film
Traditional animation with tracing paper
Production: La Fabrique Production

AWARDS
Official selection in the short film category, Cannes Film Festival
(France), 1987
Outrageous Animation tour of the United States, 1989
1st Prize, Animation Festival, Millau (France)

1989
Ciné Si
Animated TV series, 8 episodes of 12 minutes each
Cut-out silhouette animation
Content:

- La Princesse des Diamants
- Icare
- Le Garçon des Figues
- La Sorcière

- Le Manteau de la Vieille Dame

- La Reine Cruelle et le Montreur de Fabulo

- On ne saurait penser à tout

- Prince et Princesse

AWARDS
César Award nomination for Best Animated Short Film with *La Princesse des Diamants*, Paris (France), 1989
Emile Reynaud Prize for *Prince et Princesse*, National Animated Film Festival, Marly-le-Roi (France), 1989
Award for the best TV series episode, with *Prince et Princesse*, International Animated Film Festival, Ottawa (Canada), 1990
Fipresci Prize for *Le Manteau de la Vieille Dame*, International Animated Film Festival, Annecy (France), 1991

1992
La Belle Fille et le Sorcier
4-minute animated short film
Bergère qui Danse
9 min animated short film
Le Prince des Joyaux
13-minute animated short film
Cut-out silhouette animation
Production: Trans Europe Film
These three shorts are part of a series for television entitled *Les Contes de la Nuit*

1998
Kirikou et la Sorcière
70-minute animated feature film
Traditional animation
Production: Les Armateurs, co-produced with Odec Kid Cartoons, Monipoly Productions, France 3 Cinéma, Trans-Europe Films, RTBF (Télévision Belge) and Studio O

AWARDS

Grand Prize for Best Feature Film, International Animation Film Festival, Annecy (France), 1999

Best European Feature Film, British Animation Awards, London (UK), 2002

1st Prize, Children's Jury for the Best Animated Feature Film, CICFF International Children's Festival, Chicago (United States)

1st Prize, Adult Jury for the Best Animated Feature Film, CICFF International Children's Festival, Chicago (United States)

Best Feature Film, International Animated Film Festival, KROK, Kiev (Ukraine)

Cinekid Prize, International Film Festival for Children and Young Adults, Amsterdam (The Netherlands)

Best Animated Feature Film, International Festival of Montevideo (Uruguay)

Public Prize, International Film Festival of Zanzibar (Tanzania)

Public Prize (Swahili version), Lola Kenya Screen Festival, Nairobi (Kenya)

Best animated film, International Festival Cine Infantil, Santo Domingo-Santiago (Dominican Republic)

2000

Princes et Princesses

70-minute animated feature film

Cut-out silhouette animation

Production: Les Armateurs, co-produced with La Fabrique, Gebeka and Studio O

Content:

- La Princesse des Diamants

- Le Garçon des Figues

- La Sorcière

- Le Manteau de la Vieille Dame

- La Reine Cruelle et le Montreur de Fabulo
- Prince et Princesse

AWARDS
SACD Cinema Prize, Paris (France), 2000
1st Prize, Children's Jury for the Best Animated Feature Film, CICFF International Children's Festival, Chicago (United States), 2001
1st Prize, Adult Jury for the Best Animated Feature Film, CICFF International Children's Festival, Chicago (United States), 2001
Andersen Prize, International Festival of Sestri Levante (Italy), 2000
Best Film for Children, Würzburg International Filmweekend, Würzburg (Germany), 2001
OCIC Jury Special Prize, International Festival of Mar Del Plata (Argentina)
French Film Festival of Cuba, feature film category, Havana (Cuba), 2014

2005
Kirikou et les Bêtes Sauvages
Co-directed with Bénédicte Galup
75-minute animated feature film
Traditional animation
Production: Les Armateurs, co-produced with Gebeka Films, France 3 Cinéma and Studio O

AWARDS
Children's Screening, Cannes Film Festival (France), 2005
Presentation at the Museum of Modern Art (MOMA) in New York, 2006
Presentation at the Barbican Centre, London (UK), 2006
Public Prize for the Best Feature Film, International Film Festival, Wissembourg (France), 2005

International Jury Prize, Animated Film Festival, Cairo (Egypt), 2006
Public Prize, Animovie Festival, Stuttgart (Germany), 2006
1st Prize, Children's Jury for the Best Animated Feature Film, CICFF International Children's Festival, Chicago (United States)
1st Prize, Adult Jury for the Best Animated Feature Film, CICFF International Children's Festival, Chicago (United States)

2006
Azur & Asmar
101-min animated feature film
CGI animation
Production: Nord-Ouest Films, co-produced with Mac Guff Ligne, Studio O, France 3 Cinéma, Rhônes Alpes Cinéma, Artemis Productions, S2 International, Zahorimedia, Intuitions Films and Lucky Red

AWARDS
Director's Fortnight, Cannes Film Festival (France), 2006
Goya, nomination for Best Animated Film, Madrid (Spain), 2008
Best Feature Film, Children's Film Festival, London (UK), 2006
Golden Goats, Best Animated Feature Film, Ale Kino, Poznan (Poland), 2006
Grand Prize-Best Feature Film, Animafest, Zagreb (Croatia), 2007
Barrilete de Oro, Best Children Feature Film, International Film Festival Nueva Mirada for Youth and Children, Buenos Aires (Argentina), 2007
Animovi Prize for Best Animated Feature Film, International Animated Film Festival, Stuttgart (Germany), 2007
Audience Prize, Sprockets, International Children Film Festival, Toronto (Canada), 2007
Young Jury Prize, DiverCine, International Children Film Festival, Saragossa (Spain), 2014

2007
Earth Intruders, **by Björk**
Music video, 3 minutes and 53 seconds
Mixed animation techniques
Production: Little Indian Limited

2008
L'Invité aux Noces
13-min animated short film
Fixed drawings animation
Production: Nord-Ouest Films, coproduced with Studio O

2010
Dragons et Princesses
CGI animation
Animated TV series, 10 episodes of 13 minutes each
Production: Nord-Ouest Films, en co-production avec Canal+
et Studio O
Content:

- La Maîtresse des Monstres

- L'Ecolier-Sorcier

- Le Loup-Garou

- Garçon Tamtam

- Le Pont du Petit Cordonnier

- Le Garçon qui ne Mentait Jamais

- L'Elue de la Ville d'Or

- Ti Jean et la Belle-sans-Connaître

- Le Mousse et sa Chatte

- Ivan Tsarévitch et la Princesse Changeante

AWARDS
Special Award for the Best TV series, International Animation
Film Festival, ANNECY (France), 2010
Golden Star for the Best TV series, International Animation
Festival « Cinéma dans les Etoiles », Saint-Laurent le Minier
(France), 2013
Anima Mundi, International Animated Film Festival, Sao Paulo
and Rio de Janeiro (Brazil), 2010
Diverciné, International Children's Film Festival, Montevideo
(Uruguay), 2010
International Animated Film Festival, Hiroshima (Japan), 2010
International Film Festival of Abitibi-Temiscamingue, Quebec
(Canada), 2010

2011
Les Contes de la Nuit
75-minute animated feature film
CGI animation
Production: Nord-Ouest Films, co-produced with StudioCanal
and Studio O
Content:

- Le Loup-Garou

- Tijean et la Belle-Sans-Connaître

- L'Elue de la Ville d'Or

- Garçon Tamtam

- Le Garçon qui ne mentait jamais

- La Fille Biche et le Fils de l'Architecte

AWARDS
Nominated at the 61st Berlinale edition, Berlin International
Film Festival (Germany), 2011

Castello d'Argento, Castellinaria, International Children's Film Festival, Bellinzona (Switzerland), 2011

Premio Minicastellinaria, Castellinaria, International Children's Film Festival, Bellinzona (Switzerland), 2011

Special Jury Prize, International Children's Film Festival, Hyderabad (India), 2011

2012

Kirikou et les Hommes et les Femmes

90-minute animated feature film

CGI animation

Production: Les Armateurs, co-produced with MacGuff Ligne, France 3 Cinéma and Studio O

AWARDS

César, nomination for the Best Animated Film, Paris (France), 2013

Alice nella Città Festival, Rome (Italy), 2012

Children and Young People Jury Award for the Best Animated Feature Film, Nueva Mirada International Film Festival, Buenos-Aires (Argentina), 2014

Golden Kite for the Best Animated Film, Nueva Mirada International Film Festival, Buenos Aires (Argentina), 2014

2016

Ivan Tsarevich et la Princesse Changeante

CGI Animation

57-minute animated feature film

Production: Nord-Ouest Films, co-produced with Canal+ and Studio O

AWARDS

Best Children Feature Film, Carrousel International du Film, Rimouski (Quebec), 2017

Golden Reel, 8-13 years old category, Festival "Les 400 Bobines", Lisieux (France), 2017

2018
Dilili à Paris
90-minute animated feature film
Mixed techniques
Production: Nord-Ouest Films

AWARDS
Opening ceremony film of the 42nd International Animation Film Festival, Annecy (France), 2018
César Award for the Best Animated Film, Paris (France), 2019
Lumières Award for the Best Animated Film (French Golden Globes), Paris (France), 2019
Press award for the Best Feature Film, International Historical Fiction Film Festival, Plaisance du Touch (France), 2018
Creation Award, Les Lumières de Paris, International Institute for the Outreach of Paris, Paris (France), 2019
Audience Award, French Film Festival, Yokohama (Japan), 2019

2020
Pablo-Paris-Satie
4-minute live-action short film
Production: 3e Scène (Opéra National de Paris)

2022
Le Pharaon, le Sauvage et la Princesse
CGI animation
Production: Nord-Ouest Films

Bibliography

BOOKS

Asante, Molefi Kete, and Abu S. Abarry. *African Intellectual Heritage: A Book of Sources*. Philadelphia: Temple University Press, 1996.

Ayres, Brenda. *The Emperor's Old Groove: Decolonizing Disney's Magic Kingdom*. New York: Peter Lang Publishing, 2003.

Barnier, Martin, and Kira Kitsopanidou. *Le cinéma 3D: Histoire, économie, technique, esthétique*. Paris: Armand Colin, 2015.

Barthes, Roland. *Image, Music, Text*. London: Fontana Press, 1977.

Ben Nun, Yaël et al. *Michel Ocelot: Artificier de l'imaginaire*. Cinisello Balsamo: Silvana, 2021. Catalogue of the Exhibition at the Musée-Château in Annecy, 2021.

Bendazzi, Giannalberto. *Animation: A World History*. Boca Raton, FL: CRC Press, Taylor & Francis Group, 2016.

Commin, Jean-Paul, Valérie Ganne, Didier Brunner. *Kirikou et Après... 20 Ans de Cinéma d'Animation en France*. Arles: Actes Sud, 2017.

Cormon, Véronique. *Viol et renaissance*. Paris: L'Archipel, 2004.

Denis, Sébastien. *Le cinéma d'animation*. Paris: Armand Colin, 2011.

Elsaesser, Thomas. *Early Cinema: Space, Frame, Narrative*. London: British Film Institute, 1990.

Featherstone, Mike. *Undoing Culture: Globalization, Postmodernism and Identity*. New York: SAGE Publications Ltd, 1995.

Fox, Alistair, Michel Marie, and Raphaëlle Moine. *A Companion to Contemporary French Cinema*. Hoboken: John Wiley & Sons, 2015.

Furniss, Maureen. *Art in Motion: Animation Aesthetics*. New Barnet: John Libbey Publishing, 1998.

Gaudin, Antoine. *L'espace cinématographique: Esthétique et dramaturgie*. Paris: Armand Colin, 2015.

Gautier, Théophile. *Poésies Complètes*. Lost Leaf Publications, 2014.

Ionesco Eugène. *Note e contronote: Scritti sul teatro*. Torino: Einaudi, 1965.

Jouvanceau, Pierre. *Il cinema di silhouette*. Recco: Le mani, 2004.

King, C. Richard; Mary K. Bloodsworth-Lugo, and Carmen R. Lugo-Lugo. *Animating Difference: Race, Gender, and Sexuality in Contemporary Films for Children*. Lanham, Md.: Rowman & Littlefield, 2010.

Le modèle noir: de Gericault a Matisse. Paris: Musee d'Orsay/ Flammarion, 2019.

Mazumdar, Sucheta, Vasant Kaiwar, Thierry Labica. *From Orientalism to Postcolonialism. Asia, Europe and the Lineages of Difference*. New York; London: Routledge, 2009.

Mellino, Miguel. *La Critica Postcoloniale: Decolonizzazione, Capitalismo e Cosmopolitismo nei Postcolonial Studies*. Milano: Meltemi, 2021.

Ngom, Abdou. "Postcolonial Studies: An Avenue to Examining Africa's Indigenous Knowledge Systems" in *Africology: The Journal of Pan African Studies*, vol.11, no.1, December 2017, pp. 272–290.

Neupert, Richard. *French Animation History*. Oxford; Malden: Wiley-Blackwell, 2011.

Ocelot, Michel. *Tout sur Kirikou*. Paris: Seuil, 2003.

Pilling, Jayne. *Animation: 2D and Beyond*. New York: RotoVision, 2001.

Shah, Sabina. *The Portrayal of the Historical Muslim Female on Screen*. Doctoral Thesis, University of Manchester, 2017.

Schaëffner, Yves. "Kirikou ou l'innocence récompensée", in Ciné-Bulles n. 184, April, 2000.

Sifianos, Georges. *Esthétique du cinéma d'animation*. Paris; Condé-sur-Noireau: Éditions Cerf; Corlet, 2012.

Stam, Robert. *Reflexivity in Film and Literature: From Don Quixote to Jean-Luc Godard*. New York: Columbia University Press, 1992.

Tomasovic, Dick. *Le corps en abîme: Sur la figurine et le cinéma d'a-nimation*. Pertuis: Rouge Profond, 2006.

Van Brabant, Louise. *La part de l'ombre: Michel Ocelot ou la réappropriation de l'espace dans le film de silhouettes*. Master Thesis, Université de Liège, Liège, 2017.

Varela, Stéphanie. La peinture animée. Paris: L'Harmatan, 2010.

Vimenet, Pascal. *Un abécédaire de la fantasmagorie*. Paris: l'Harmatan, 2015.

Vogler, Christopher. *Il viaggio dell'Eroe: La struttura del mito ad uso di scrittori di narrativa e di cinema*. Roma: Dino Audino, 2020.

Zipes, Jack. *The Enchanted Screen: The Unknown History of Fairy Tale Films*. New York; London: Routledge, 2010.

Zipes, Jack, Pauline Grennhill, and Kendra Magnus-Johnston. *Fairy-Tale Films Beyond Disney: International Perspectives*. New York; London: Routledge, 2015.

INTERVIEWS AND ARTICLES

"Abd Al Malik parle du dessin animé Kirikou". Interview by Brut in occasion of the Festival Lumière, 2018. https://www.youtube.com/watch?v=SHyO_wDOteI, last consulted on September 27, 2022.

"An Extensive Personal Interview with Director Michel Ocelot", in *GhibliWorld*, August 29, 2008. https://web.archive.org/web/20080829185726/http:/www.ghibliworld.com/michel_ocelot_interview.html, last consulted on December 10, 2022.

Apostolou, Fotini. "Cultural Translations: Transcending Boundaries in Michel Ocelot's Animated Film Azur et Asmar (2006)", in *Communication, Politics & Culture*, University of Thessaloniki, 2009, pp. 96–113.

ASIFA's Official Website. https://asifa.net, last consulted on September 27, 2022.

"Azur e Asmar. Cartella stampa." Lucky Red. https://docplayer.it/amp/9633544-Presenta-azur-e-asmar-un-film-di-michel-ocelot.html, last consulted on December 29, 2022.

"Azur & Asmar. Dossier de presse." Nord-Ouest Films. https://www.michelocelot.fr/attachments/DP_AA.pdf, last consulted on December 29, 2022.

"Azur and Asmar Review", in *Iridium Eye Reviews*, November 7, 2020. https://iridiumeye.wordpress.com/2020/11/07/azur-and-asmar-review/, last consulted on December 29, 2022.

Baker, Rob, and Ellen Draper. "If One Thing Stands, Another Will Stand Beside It: An Interview with Chinua Achebe", in *Parabola* 173, Fall 1992, pp. 19–27.

Bazou, Sébastien. "Princes et Princesses: Les contes de fées revisités", in *ArteFake*, January 5, 2011. https://web.archive.org/web/20110105122330/http:/www.artefake.com/spip.php?article125, last consulted on November 6, 2022.

Boisseau, Rosita. "Kirikou, sur scène plus vrai que nature", in *Télérama*, October 10, 2007. https://www.telerama.fr/scenes/20917-kirikou_plus_vrai_que_nature.php, last consulted on November 6, 2022.

Cailleau, Emma, Gérard Moreau, and Michèle Barrault. "'Dilili à Paris' ou l'escamotage de la colonisation", in *Billets d'Afrique*, January 26, 2019. https://survie.org/billets-d-afrique/2019/283-decembre-2018-janvier-2019/article/dilili-a-paris-ou-l-escamotage-de-la-colonisation, last consulted on March 18, 2023.

Cassiau-Haurie, Christophe. "Enfants de Kirikou. Quand les dessinateurs africains font leur cinéma", in *Africultures*, April 1, 2005. http://africultures.com/enfants-de-kirikou-7475/?utm_source=newsletter&utm_medium=email&utm_campaign=538#prettyPhoto, last consulted on September 27, 2022.

Ciment, Gilles. "Kirikou et la Sorcière de Michel Ocelot", in *Positif* n. 455, January 1999. http://gciment.free.fr/cencacritiquekirikou.htm, last consulted on September 27, 2022.

Cole, Teju, "The White-Savior Industrial Complex", in *The Atlantic*, March 21, 2012. https://www.theatlantic.com/international/archive/2012/03/the-white-savior-industrial-complex/254843/, last consulted on December 29, 2022.

Crenshaw, Kimberlé "Mapping the Margins: Intersectionality, Identity Politics, and Violence against Women of Color", in *Stanford Law Review*, vol. 43, no. 6 (Jul., 1991), pp. 1241–1299.

"Critique D'autres films", in Libération, July, 20, 2011. https://www.liberation.fr/cinema/2011/07/20/d-autres-films_750240/, last consulted on December 10, 2022.

Debruge, Peter. "Film Review: 'Dilili in Paris'", in *Variety*, October 4, 2019. https://variety.com/2019/film/reviews/dilili-in-paris-review-1203358672/, last consulted on March 18, 2023.

"Dilili à Paris. Cartella stampa." Nord-Ouest Films. http://files.spazioweb.it/74/3f/743f4b65-0b27-4e62-b0ba-907bd1c10e25.pdf, last consulted on March 18, 2023.

"Dilili à Paris. Dossier de presse." Nord-Ouest Films. https://www.michelocelot.fr/attachments/DILILI_A_PARIS_DP_V2_9.pdf, last consulted on March 18, 2023.

Dobroiu, Ştefan. "Review: Dilili in Paris", in *Cineuropa*, October 16, 2019. https://cineuropa.org/en/newsdetail/379942/, last consulted on March 18, 2023.

"Dragons et Princesses. Dossier de presse." https://www.michelocelot.fr/attachments/DP_DP.pdf, last consulted on December 10, 2022.

Ezzakhrajy, Myriam. "Michel Ocelot. Un féministe engagé", in *Femmes du Maroc*, April 26, 2019. https://femmesdumaroc.com/archives/michel-ocelot-un-feministe-engage, last consulted on March 18, 2023.

Fagerholm Matt, "Reviews: Dilili in Paris", in *Roger Erbert.com*, October 04, 2019. https://www.rogerebert.com/reviews/dilili-in-paris-2019, last consulted on March 18, 2023.

Floquet, Pierre. "CinémAnimations", in *CinémAction*, n.123, Condé-sur-Noireau: Corlet, 2007.

Griseri, Carlo. "Intervista al regista francese Michel Ocelot", in *Cinemaitaliano.info*, December 15, 2012. https://www.cinemaitaliano.info/news/16029/sotto18-michel-ocelot-il-papa-di-kiriku.html, last consulted on September 27, 2022.

Guedj, Philippe. "Dilili à Paris divise le Festival d'Annecy", in *Le Point Pop*, June 12, 2018. https://www.lepoint.fr/pop-culture/dilili-a-paris-divise-le-festival-d-annecy-12-06-2018-2226362_2920.php, last consulted on March 18, 2023.

Guillen, Michael. "Animation: Azur & Asmar. A Few Questions for Michel Ocelot", in *Screenanarchy*, March 9 2009. https://screenanarchy.com/2009/03/animation-azur-asmara-few-questions-for-michel-ocelot.html, last consulted on December 10, 2022.

Gunning, Tom. "Fantasmagorie et fabrication de l'illusion", in *Cinémas*, vol.14, no. 1, 2003, pp. 67–89. https://vpn.gw.ulg.ac.be/fr/revues/cine/2003-v14-n1- cine751/0089958ar/,DanaInfo=www.erudit.org,SSL+, last consulted on November 6, 2022.

Hind O. "«Azur et Asmar est inspiré de l'Algérie...» Entretien avec Michel Ocelot", in *L'Expression*, December 24, 2007. https://www.djazairess.com/fr/lexpression/48238, last consulted on December 29, 2022.

Interview by Giannalberto Bendazzi on the occasion of the 11th edition of AniFest, Teplice, Czech Republic, April 26 - May 1, 2012. https://www.youtube.com/watch?v=08SL0atjN8s, last consulted on November 6, 2022.

"Interview dessinée. Michel Ocelot". Interview by FM-Institut français du Maroc, 2019. https://www.youtube.com/watch?v=Z6vXjyHr4EQ, last consulted on September 27, 2022.

"Interview de Michel Ocelot, à l'occasion des 70 ans du Festival de Cannes." https://www.youtube.com/watch?v=SuX0lK6GSwE, last consulted on December 29, 2022.

"Inteview with Michel Ocelot. Interview conducted by Marie d'Harcourt". Opéra National de Paris, 2020. https://www.youtube.com/watch?v=k9hoi2MWwfE, last consulted on March 18, 2023.

Interview with Michel Ocelot on the occasion of the 10th edition of Mon premier Festival, 22-28 October 2014. https://www.youtube.com/watch?v=HZokp8pcQ9M, last consulted on November 6, 2022.

"Interview with Michel Ocelot of Dilili and Paris Time Trip, which Captures Beautiful Paris in a Realistic Movie", in Gigazine, August 12, 2019. https://gigazine.net/gsc_news/en/20190812-dilili-paris-michel-ocelot-interview/, last consulted on March 18, 2023.

"Kabongo le Griot, Studio Pictoon." Interview to Pierre Sauvalle by Pour Une Meilleur Afrik, 2015. https://www.youtube.com/watch?v=2HlOgAHwAko, last consulted on September 27, 2022.

"Kirikou et la Sorcière. Dossier de presse." Les Armateurs.

James, Alison. "Some Nix Kirikou Due to Nudity", in *Variety*, December 26, 2005.

Labesse, Patrick. "Manu Dibango meets Kirikou. France's Hot New Film Soundtrack", in *RFI Musique*, December 27, 2005. http://www1.rfi.fr/musiqueen/articles/072/article_7653.asp, last consulted on September 27, 2022.

"Le Pharaon, le Sauvage et la Princesse." Interview by Alexis Clément on Tuesday, June 14, during the Festival International du Film d'Animation d'Annecy, France, 2022. https://www.youtube.com/watch?v=lx4ePSn2ZOk&list=PLF-P8Sj_MG4UCpCiFAUQD0dYRP2wmI03b&index=1, last consulted on November 6, 2022.

"Les Contes de la Nuit. Dossier de presse." Nord-Ouest Films. https://medias.unifrance.org/medias/173/10/68269/presse/les-contes-de-la-nuit-dossier-de-presse-francais.pdf, last consulted on December 10, 2022.

"Le zootrope épatant", in *Fluide Glacial*, n. 66. Paris: Audie, December 1981, pp. 42–43.

Leffrer, Rebecca. "'Tales of the Night' Director Michel Ocelot Brings Animated 3D to Competition Field (Berlin)", in *The Hollywood Reporter*, February 12, 2011, https://www.hollywoodreporter.com/movies/movie-news/tales-night-director-michel-ocelot-98968/, last consulted on December 29, 2022.

Lorfèvre, Alain. "'Dilili à Paris', un conte maladroit un brin moralisateur", in *La Libre*, October 24, 2018. https://www.lalibre.be/culture/cinema/2018/10/24/dilili-a-paris-un-conte-maladroit-un-brin-moralisateur-YSAPOVS6PNC4BJNKMQAWJUWPKQ/, last consulted on March 18, 2023.

Lussier, Marc-André. "Les contes de la nuit: Le sorcier fait son cinéma", in *La Presse*, Anjou: La Presse, March 3, 2012. https://www. lapresse.ca/cinema/nouvelles/201207/17/01-4544961-les-contes-de-la-nuit-le-sorcier-fait-son-cinema.php, last consulted on November 6, 2022.

Mandelbaum, Jacques. "L'enfant sauvage et la beauté du mal", in *Le Monde*, December 10, 1998.

Master-Class by Michel Ocelot moderated by Vanessa Tonnini on the occasion of Movie Up 2020, October 27, 2018. https://en. unifrance.org/news/15452/michel-ocelot-gives-a-master-class-in-rome, last consulted on Dicember 10, 2022.

"Michel Ocelot aux Cinemas Studio in Tours, France. Film Presentation: *Ivan Tsarevitch et la Princesse Changeante* aux cinémas Studio de Tours." October 2, 2016. https://www.youtube. com/watch?v=jQgrOIpfRtc&ab_channel=CinemasStudioTours, last consulted on December 10, 2022.

"Michel Ocelot: De l'ombre à la lumiere." Interview by Laurent Valière and Stéphane Landfried on the occasion of the 73rd Congrès Dauville 2018: Hommage à Michel Ocelot.

"Michel Ocelot en Afrique." Interview conducted by Juliette Binoche on May 3, 2021, during the third edition of the Branche & Ciné Festival, organized by the Office National des Forêts. https://www.youtube. com/watch?v=6TWx-cRTGag, last consulted on November 6, 2022.

"Michel Ocelot: Enchanteur de l'animation à la française." Interview conducted by Robin Gatto on June 05, 2001. https://www. filmfestivals.com/fr/blog/editor/michel_ocelot_enchanteur_de_ lanimation_a_la_francaise, last consulted on November 6, 2022.

"Michel Ocelot, l'inventeur." Conversation between Michel Ocelot and Hervé Joubert-Laurencin at the 4th professional meeting on animated film writing in Fontevraud, October 9, 2015.

Michel Ocelot's Official Website. https://www.michelocelot.fr, last consulted on April 2, 2023.

Mitchell, Elvis. "Can-Do African Boy Wins and Evil Sorceress Loses", in *The New York Times*, February 18, 2000. https://www.nytimes.com/ 2000/02/18/movies/film-review-can-do-african-boy-wins-and-evil-sorceress-loses.html, last consulted on September 27, 2022.

Mtshali, Seni. *Colonial Stereotypes: Kirikou and the Sorceress as Representation of French views of West Africa*. University of Witwatersrand, Johannesburg, 2012. https://www.researchgate. net/publication/260082287, last consulted on September 27, 2022.

Mouton-Dubosc, Xavier, and Thomas Berthelon. "Michel Ocelot (Kirikou): «Je veux vous faire du bien.»", in *ActuaBd*, October 18, 2012. https://www.actuabd.com/Michel-Ocelot-Kirikou-Je-veux-vous, last consulted on December 29, 2022.

Mury, Cécile. "Le gamin déluré enthousiasme l'Afrique", in *Télérama* n. 2885 April 30, 2005. https://www.c-n-a.org/articles/Telerama_Kirikou.htm, last consulted on September 27, 2022.

Neupert, Richard. "Kirikou and the animated figure/body", in *Studies in French Cinema*, 8(1), Taylor & Francis, 2008, pp. 41–56.

Nicholas, Lynnette "#NYICFF19 Review: 'Dilili in Paris'", in *BlackGirlNerd*. https://blackgirlnerds.com/nyicff19-review-dilili-in-paris/, last consulted on March 18, 2023.

Obejas, Achy et al. "The Dark Side of Degas", in *Chicago Tribune*, December 24, 1996. https://www.chicagotribune.com/news/ct-xpm-1996-12-24-9612240041-story.html, /, last consulted on March 18, 2023.

Oury, Antoine. "Kirikou et la Sorcière, d'après les contes africains recueillis par François-Victor Équilbecq", in *Actualité*, June 8, 2017. https://actualitte.com/article/24693/bande-annonce/kirikou-et-la-sorciere-d-apres-les-contes-africains-recueillis-par-francois-victor-equilbecq, last consulted on September 27, 2022.

Paternò, Cristiana. "Michel Ocelot", in *CinecittàNews*, October 17, 2006. https://news.cinecitta.com/IT/it-it/news/54/61972/michel-ocelot.aspx, last consulted on December 29, 2022.

Provencher, Normand. "'Dilili à Paris', la fable féministe de Michel Ocelot", in *Le Soleil*, December 6, 2018. https://www.lesoleil.com/2018/12/07/dilili-a-paris-la-fable-feministe-de-michel-ocelot-425f7fe3a1731d993304e6b432f7bd8c/, last consulted on March 18, 2023.

"Rencontre avec Michel Ocelot (Créateur de Kirikou)". Africa N°1. https://www.youtube.com/watch?v=zqgCJU8u3dg, last consulted on September 27, 2022.

Rigouste, Paul. "Les Contes de la nuit (2011): Le sexisme archaïque de Michel Ocelot", in *Le cinéma est politique*, July 26, 2012.

Rosaldo, Renato. "Ideology, Place, and People without Culture", in *Place and Voice in Anthropological Theory*, vol. 3, no. 1, February 1988, pp. 77–87.

Russell, Jamie. "Kirikou and the Sorceress", in *BBC*, June 23, 2003. https://www.bbc.co.uk/films/2003/06/23/kirikou_and_the_sorceress_2003_review.shtml, last consulted on September 27, 2022.

Sifianos, George. "Une technique idéale", in *Positif*, Paris: Scope, 1991, pp. 102–104.

Ugolini, Chiara. "'Dilili a Parigi', Michel Ocelot: 'Un cartoon femminista? Umanista, direi'", in *La Repubblica*, April 29, 2019. https://www.repubblica.it/spettacoli/cinema/2019/04/23/news/_dilili_a_parigi_michel_ocelot_un_film_femminista_umanista_direi_-224195191/, last consulted on March 18, 2023.

Zeneise, Gatto. "Esclusiva: intervista a Michel Ocelot", in *afNews.info*, October 1, 2014. https://www.afnews.info/wordpress/2014/10/01/esclusiva-intervista-a-michel-ocelot/, last consulted on December 29, 2022.

DOCUMENTARIES

La Belle Epoque de Michel Ocelot. Documentary by Théo Caillat and Charles Murat, Studio Basho, France, 2020.

Les Trésors Cachés de Michel Ocelot. DVD, Nord-Ouest, Studio O, France, 2008.

Michel Ocelot. Ma vie d'artiste. Documentary by Letop Mags, France, 2015.

Portrait de Michel Ocelot. Documentary by Véronique Martin, France, 2006.

Index

Printed in the United States
by Baker & Taylor Publisher Services